THE GARDEN ENTRUSTED TO ME

The Garden Entrusted to Me

Essays on Poetry and the Writing Life

Robert Bly

Edited by Thomas R. Smith

WHITE PINE PRESS / BUFFALO, NEW YORK

White Pine Press
P.O. Box 236
Buffalo, NY 14201
www.whitepine.org

Publication of this book was supported by public funds from the New York State Council on the Arts, with the support of Governor Kathy Hochul and the New York State Legislature, a State Agency.

Acknowledgements: See page 202

Book Design: Elaine LaMattina

Printed and bound in the United States of America.

ISBN 978-1-945680-85-4

Library of Congress Control Number: 2024952166

CONTENTS

FOR RUTH BLY

INTRODUCTION
THE PLAYFULNESS OF HIS LABOR: ROBERT BLY'S LIFE IN POETRY

Working as Robert Bly's assistant for more than three decades, I occupied a unique position for viewing the full range of his literary activity. Poems, essays, plays, op-eds, and reviews — to say nothing of Robert's ample correspondence — flowed through my typist's fingers to manifest on the page. As the years passed, I became persistently aware of certain key writings that, once published in some journal or anthology, sank from notice and were not preserved in any of Robert's books. Often these writings focused on the specific details of Robert's life and practice.

In his better known critical essays, Robert typically praised poets he admired — Tomas Tranströmer, James Wright, and Jane Hirshfield are a few — or insulted poets he disliked, which in his combative younger days were many: James Dickey stands out as a recipient of some of Robert's most devastating attacks. Conspicuously, Robert had seldom discussed in any detail his own practice.

To remedy that lack, I compiled a first version of this book in 2017, when Robert had come to the end of his active writing life, and pitched my idea to him and his wife Ruth. They approved and gave me the go-ahead to pursue my project. Both preferred as title *The Garden Entrusted to Me,* one of a list I'd drawn from the essays. The speaker in Antonio Machado's poem quoted in the title, translated by Robert as "The Wind, One Brilliant Day," confesses that he has let his inner "garden" languish.

> "I have no roses; I have no flowers,
> All the flowers in my garden are dead. . . ."
>
> The wind left . . . I wept, I said to my soul,
> "What have you done with the garden entrusted to me?"

I doubt that any reader of this book will accuse Robert of that speaker's neglect of the literary "garden entrusted to him."

These essays, originally scattered across miscellaneous books and periodicals, some previously unpublished, concentrate on Robert's personal approach to the art and music of poetry. I believe they can be of great value to beginning and seasoned poets alike, as well as to general readers who wish to better understand the biographical, cultural, intellectual, and spiritual wellsprings of Robert's ever-evolving and unfolding artistry. In this introduction I'll alternate between referring to him as Robert or Bly, depending on the tone of the context.

I.

Part One of *The Garden Entrusted to Me* includes some of Bly's most directly autobiographical writings, including his strangely neglected "Being a Lutheran Boy-God in Minnesota" from Chester G. Anderson's 1976 anthology, *Growing Up in Minnesota.* Bly's sometimes nostalgic account of his farm origins in western Minnesota and early exposure to poetry as a high school student is as near as he ever came to autobiography. His tribute to his father Jacob's moral rectitude in helping to secure the release of a farm hand unjustly imprisoned for a minor offense is especially revelatory. In the elder Bly's example we unearth the early roots of Robert's own moral outrage at social injustice and war in both his poetry and his peace activism, and possibly in his men's work as well:

> To be able to respect your father is such a beautiful thing! I learned then that the indignation of the solitary man is the stone pin that connects this world to the next. The more easy-going businessmen in Madison, who had so many friends, would have left Garth sitting in his cell for twenty years. They would have been afraid to put their hands into the web of social friendships, afraid the web would not be repaired overnight, or that the spider of loneliness would bite them. I learned too that when you have been unselfish, people respond not in words but by feeding you. I learned so much from that one story! We don't need to read books on ethics or to see documentaries on television; one moral example will do for a lifetime.

Bly's anecdotal accounts of his years of struggle before rising to prominence in American poetry tease the reader with yearning for what he might have made of a full-blown memoir. In the rich, brief essay "Tigers and Horses" he relates that after two years in New York City as a young man living "like Noah, sending out a crow each day," "a blessed thing happened":

> I walked along in New York, among thousands, and a man stopped me and asked, "Are you a poet?" No one could have given me a greater gift. He turned out to be an exiled Polish

> poet, hoping to find someone who could translate his poems. But he had picked me out of a hundred thousand, and made me feel that my secret was known, and I belonged to a long line of ignored young poets.

"The tigers of wrath," William Blake wrote, "are wiser than the horses of instruction." Bly's prose is never more alive and sensitive to the movement of the psyche among the astonishments and disappointments of this world than when he is carried to his "dark place by dragons or tigers, not by the horses of instruction." Later, as a teacher, Bly distinguished himself as a fiery free tiger intellect instead of a plodding establishment plowhorse.

Another essay, "When Literary Life Was Still Piled Up in a Few Places," a tribute to Paul Engle at the Iowa Writers Workshop, gives tantalizing glimpses of Bly's post-New-York stint at the University of Iowa. He tells the lovely story of rescuing two baby Great Horned Owls from the Mississippi River flats and being asked to show them to Engle's third-grade daughter's class. Twenty years later he hears an apocryphal account of bringing a snake in a gunny sack to his class at the Workshop and "whenever someone began to criticize a poem of mine, I would take out the snake and lay it on the table." He observes that "the human proclivities for envy, projection, and malice had altered the tale of two half-grown owls in a cardboard box in the third grade to a snake in a gunny sack in a graduate school classroom. So it is."

2.

In Part Two of this book remembrance gives way to Bly's views on the vocation and discipline of poetry. "What the Image Can Do," published in the early 1980s in Donald Hall's anthology *Claims for Poetry*, while moderating Bly's earlier emphasis on the image still makes a strong case for the power of the image to bring "moistness" to a poem. Bly's praise in this essay directed many readers to the English critic Owen Barfield's *Poetic Diction*, from which he quotes extensively. "The power of the image," Bly says, amplifying Barfield, "is the power of seeing resemblances. That discipline is essential to the growth of intelligence, to everyone's intelligence, but especially to the poet's intelligence."

In 2001 Minnesota's McKnight Foundation named Bly their Distinguished Artist of the year, celebrating his seventy-fifth birthday by funding the publication of an issue of *The Thousands,* a reprise of Bly's pioneering magazine *The Fifties* and *The Sixties.* Featuring "Six Disciplines that Intensify Poetry" and an essay on Jane Hirshfield (by, in keeping with the magazine's tradition, the pseudonymous "Abou Ben Adam"), *The Thousands* Number One was a feast for those who knew and loved Bly's earlier publication.

"Six Disciplines" is one of Bly's last comprehensive statements of his philosophy of poetry. He still places a high value on image and metaphor, but these new "disciplines" also include "excess" and "the ancient friendship between sounds." In "Six Disciplines" we find a first mention of what Bly calls "sound particles" such as *ar* and *or* and *un*:

> The language experts, who have very little sense of language, call them phonemes. Please forget that right away. Calling them sound particles is OK for now. . . . They are really little creatures—*in* and *am* and *el* and *il* and *en*. A sound friendship, or a sound-urn contains the delicate, easily destroyed artifacts of music. A sound particle or being is the union of a heavily veiled vowel and a consonant, the one leaning on the other, so to speak, two friends who are never parted, who always sing the same little tune, no matter how it's spelled.

"The Vocation of Poetry," also included in this section, was worked up from a 2004 lecture and appears here for the first time.

3.

Part Three of this book carries us deeper into the technical heart of Bly's practice. Readers may be surprised at the concentration on form in these essays, remembering that the contentious mid-period Bly often disparaged the writers' workshops' fixation on craft concerns. In 1981's "Educating the Rider and the Horse" Bly admits that he was relatively late in coming to his reconsideration of form: "If I have been wrong in that, then I need to find a way to speak of form so that its wild or intense quality becomes clear."

Somewhat ironically, given the long-limbed Whitmanic line he has frequently employed, Bly sees little formal coherence in Whitman:

> If we imagine one of Whitman's long poems as an animal, it would be an animal about a mile and half long with not enough

> bone structure between head and tail, big in the stomach, and so cumbersome it would be killed by the first lion that noticed it on the grassy plain.

This statement can also be viewed as implied criticism of some of Bly's own poems, including his ambitious long poem "Sleepers Joining Hands," with which he seems to have never been completely satisfied.

Form, he says, "is something playful which actually increases one's chances of remaining alive in a dangerous world. . . . Only creatures with achieved form live, whether it be a stingray or a hummingbird or some snake with elegantly repeated scales going on for ten feet."

Like other poets of his generation, Bly first got his poetic feet wet in the iambic pentameter dominating English poetic tradition. His resistance to that tradition in the 1950s prompted a search beyond English models for fresh expressive possibilities and content in world poetries as varied as the Spanish and the Chinese. The unloosening of American poetry that the so-called Deep Image brought in the 1960s, in tandem with the social challenges of the anti-war and the Civil Rights movements, further enflamed Bly's antagonism toward suffocating received forms.

It's fair to say that in those years Bly's position was widely viewed as anti-form. Donald Hall, Bly's best poet friend and critic, certainly recognized that alienation from establishment models. In 1974 he wrote that Bly seemed "mostly unaware" of "the motion and the feel of language." He adds, "If Bly could write his poems in amino acids and bird calls, he would just as lief; the spirit matters to him, and not the shoulders of consonants." We don't know exactly how Bly took Hall's assessment of his disregard for language, but it seems likely that beneath Bly's vocal disdain for formal concerns an intense awareness of formal challenges was simmering.

The 1989 essay "A Playful Look at Form" is practically a gloss on the ideas about form and sound Hall set down in his influential essay "Goatfoot Milktongue Twinbird." Here and elsewhere the reader will recognize Hall's impact on the evolution of Bly's approach to form.

Another profound influence was a slender, provocative volume from 1991 by the musical scholar Joscelyn Godwin, *The Mystery of the Seven Vowels: In Theory and Practice*. Godwin, also an authority on Western esoteric spiritual traditions, examines the many and diverse creative systems linking vowel sounds to planets, chakras, colors, and musical tones. Imaginative rather than definitive, Godwin's survey may have acted as a catalyst to Bly's exploration of the significance and power of sound in poetry.

Two essays here, "Praising the Seven Holy Vowels" and "The Long Vowels," cast direct light on the sound-music of Bly's later poems. The former, published in the Minnesota journal *The Hungry Mind Review* in 1997, makes clear Bly's debt to Godwin. Bly is especially struck by the idea that "each major vowel affects the physical body; and the body responds by trying to move in a certain way." Always an advocate for bringing the physical body into the poem, Bly sees these esoteric and largely forgotten systems as a means to anchor the poem in the physical for both poet and listener: "In much poetry, the live limbs of the lines, so to speak, reside utterly in the long vowels."

What to do, he ponders, with the fact that the English language has "an immense number of short vowels in comparison to the number of long vowels"? Bly suggests attention to the small combinations of vowel and consonant he calls "sound particles" as "more congenial to the English language" rather than a strict emphasis on long vowel sounds. He gives his love poem "Ferns" as example of lines seeded by the sound particle *er:*

> It was among ferns I learned about eternity.
> Below your belly there's a curly place.
> Through you I learned to love the ferns on that bank,
> And the curve the deer's hoof leaves in sand.

Bly's greatest pleasure in poetry, he now writes, derives from "the intentful chiming of sounds, from worship of the sound particles and the Seven Holy Vowels."

Bly steps even farther into technical intricacy in "The Long Vowels," appearing here for the first time. In 1995 Bly was invited to work with Galway Kinnell's students at New York University, and it's fascinating to see where he went with that teaching. Anticipating "Praising the Seven Holy Vowels" by two years, this lecture transcription offers a rare glimpse of Bly in a formal educational setting. I've done some limited editing with Robert's approval to avoid unnecessary repetition of other essays in this section. "Whenever we talk of human life, we are talking about participation and separation," he tells the students. "I want to say now that it is sound and only sound that holds the secret of participation in poetry."

I've also included here a series of short commentaries on Bly's ghazals written for the *Minneapolis StarTribune*/Minnesota Public Radio's *Talking Volumes* series in December 2001. Appearing daily for a week, these pieces each recall the creative genesis and development of one of the ghazals in Bly's 2001 collection *The Night Abraham Called to the Stars.* Further illuminating the method of these sometimes elusive poems, which would constitute the major portion of Bly's poetic output for the next decade, Bly shares a favorite practice in "Writing a Poem While Listening to Music."

4.

Bly's *Paris Review* interview conducted in 2001 by fellow poet and teacher Francis Quinn concludes this collection. With agility and grace, this lengthy interview navigates biographical, artistic, and philosophical themes of Bly's life and work. Along with "Being a Lutheran Boy-God in Minnesota," with which we began this book, these two pieces together form the core of the small body of actual autobiography Bly committed to print.

I'll resist quoting at length from the interview, and touch only briefly on a point or two following the discussion of formal matters raised in this introduction. Although Bly saw traditional form as inadequate to poetry's engagement with contemporary realities, he felt that modernity's substitute, free verse, had struck a dead end as well. "One of our jobs these days," he bluntly tells Quinn, "is to escape from free verse."

What exactly does escaping from free verse mean to Robert Bly circa 2001? Having stated the importance of vowel and sound particle, Bly argues for "chiming," which sounds a lot like internal rhyme or the near- or off-rhyming that gives formal poets more room to move in rhyme-poor English:

> Most good poems have repeating sounds. But one can make chiming into a sort of principle. If the chiming sound returns three times, it becomes a tune. Then the whole stanza turns to music.

It should be obvious that Bly was never really against or indifferent to form or craft; his issue was instead with the moribund language typically used to describe it. As he said in a trenchant 1972 interview, "American craft-talk has been connected with the idea of the poem as a dead object. . . . But the whole genius of modern poetry lies in its grasp of flowing psychic energy."

As noted earlier, the idea for this book grew out of the thousands of hours I spent with Robert as his assistant and from things I heard him say and write over a thirty-year period. All that time I was myself a working poet, and learning from Robert up close was in itself a complete literary education.

Looking back in my journals, I was startled to be reminded that two essays in this collection, respectively "When Literary Life Was Still Piled Up in a Few Places" and the commentary on "Snowbanks North of the House," were dictated on the same day, Friday, August 16, 1996, and that that in fact happened to be the order in which I placed them in this book. Robert, on a good day, was a tiger of energy, but even so the seventeen typed pages he "composed on the tongue" that day were a prodigy that staggered me as my fingers raced to keep up with his lightning sentences. Given the retrospective nature of both essays, it doesn't surprise me that a continuity of mood kept them linked here in the order in which Robert delivered them.

The essay for Paul Engle was one of Robert's first attempts to reach back into his vast journals, in this case from 1954, for material. His great energy that day was in part due to relief for a breather between drafts of his labor-intensive prose volume *The Sibling Society*. Robert said he could never have accomplished that day's work with the immediate pressure of the prose book upon him. He added that he couldn't have done the Engle essay without my alertness and interest as a motivating factor. I did not look that gift compliment in the mouth but took it as offered.

In my time with Robert, it was my privilege to clerically midwife a wealth of important, original, and instructive writings on the art of poetry and the life of the poet. Over those years I realized I was mentally compiling a private anthology of essays and commentaries Robert scattered like the sower he was on the fertile ground of American poetry. Now at last that anthology is no longer mine only. In his long career Robert never stopped moving long enough to give a full personal accounting of his path as a poet, his stewardship of the "garden entrusted to him." I hope this volume will at least partly address that lack and inspire poets and readers who long to learn more about the nourishing "labor of the playfulness," as he puts it, as well as the serious playfulness of Robert's labor of poetry.

* * *

The radiant personal tribute Jane Hirshfield has contributed as afterword to this book underscores the posthumous nature of its publication. *The Garden Entrusted to Me* is the first volume to be published under Robert's name since his death on November 21, 2021, a month short of what would have been his 95th birthday. I trust there will be others.

Robert died at a time when the COVID pandemic had begun to wane. I visited him every few weeks during those months. Thanks to Robert's wife and faithful caregiver Ruth, he was able to remain in the house where they'd lived on Girard Avenue for the past three decades. Robert still took evident enjoyment in his life, circumscribed as it had become, still asking for his morning coffee, taking pleasure in visitors coming to sing or read poetry for him, radiating some original joy in being alive until almost the end.

A year later, the house put on the market and Ruth relocating to California to be near her daughter Wesley, Minneapolis saw an estate state unlike any other, tables laden with books, chapbooks, broadsides, signed editions, art works, and all manner of Bly remnants large and small. Almost indecent to be picking those luminous bones of Robert's literary corpus, but pick them I did, along with the multitudes who lined up all down the block to enter that poetry treasure castle. I felt a kind of exquisite agony standing amidst Robert's smoldering plenty, not giving up having wished that it could go on forever.

NOTES

"The Wind, One Brilliant Day"
There are different versions of this translation, and I've used here the last one Robert published in 2004 in *The Winged Energy of Delight: Selected Translations*

"Being a Lutheran Boy-God in Minnesota"
Chester G. Anderson, editor, *Growing Up in Minnesota: Ten Writers Remember Their Childhoods*, University of Minnesota Press, Minneapolis, MN, 1976

"In 1974 he wrote that Bly seemed 'mostly unaware'"
Donald Hall, "Notes on Robert Bly and *Sleepers Joining Hands*," in *Goatfoot Milktongue Twinbird: Interviews, Essays, and Notes on Poetry, 1970-1976*, The University of Michigan Press, Ann Arbor, 1978, p. 137

"As he said in a trenchant 1972 interview"
Robert Bly, "Craft Interview: With Mary Jane Fortunato and Cornelia P. Draves, and with Paul Zweig and Saul Galin," in *Talking All Morning*, The University of Michigan Press, Ann Arbor, 1980, p. 200

I.

THE LIFE OF POETRY

BEING A LUTHERAN BOY-GOD IN MINNESOTA

An old milk delivery wagon my uncle had used once to deliver milk all around town stood near the smokehouse. Some disaster had happened to him—I didn't know what it was at the time, and the milk wagon stood there floating, pale, deserted by human beings. And the smokehouse had walls of stone, all smoky and blacked on the inside, the roof a frail contraption of boards, soaked in wood smoke as if in ocean water, but frail and liable to die compared to the walls.

There were six people in the household. The only children were my brother, James, and I. He was a year and a half older, but we began school together and were in the same grade. My mother worked at the courthouse during the day, and so a wonderful woman named Marie Schmidt took care of us for years. My father always had a hired man, and one, Art Nelson, was with us for eight or nine years.

My father wearing a large black coat stands near the windmill, holding a baby up over the snow; it is my brother or myself. The windmill is stark, my father has had to become a man too soon. At sixteen he quit school, being the oldest son, to work. Always around him there was a high exhilaration, pursued by grief and depression, and a tough mother, who believed in rules. He had a gift for deep feeling. Other men bobbed like corks around his silence, and around his swift decisions; that did not bring him more company, but did help carry the burdens higher up the mountain. His heart beat very fast, and he felt himself tied to this earth. At church he kept his arms crossed over his chest. He had the sturdiest respect, grained and unplaned, for some men and women; when others were mentioned, you were astounded to find out how little he thought of them. A brooding secrecy lifted the short sentences he said. And he stubbornly refused to be carried away on easy judgments that serve to bind a company together and resemble stones bouncing over the surface of the water. He preferred weight, even if the stone sank all the way to the bottom.

* * *

And those hot days, the top of the threshing machine hot and shaking, my father standing there with legs wide, how good to feel all that shaking beneath you, coming up through the soles of the feet and the legs, the horses stamping to scare flies, as they wait for their load to go, the earthy and good machine, friendly to man except when it took a finger or an arm, its great front choppers coming out and down, to warn the bundles their time had come.

Our time has come! It is all right. How good it is to give the end of it all away, to let life go . . . so that the female shapes floating in the sky can be told what they already know, that waterfalls are wet, that water pours down, that we too are unassimilatable by objects, and we are born to sail sideways through the spaces between objects, between stars, between our deaths — and how often we have died . . . so many times eaten by wild animals, as we waited, dozing, beneath a tree, the water gourd and dried meat nearby, the tribe gone on to the hive, and all our anguish in this life is a sideways step in the darkness, slipping between two heavy posts we cannot see . . . so on the threshing machine, the legs always gave thanks to the Father, the Son, and the Holy Ghost. . . .

* * *

My brother and I went to a country school. It had one room, the teachers were just and kind, and I liked everything that happened to me there. By the time we started, most of the country schools had closed, and District 94, where I went from the third grade on, was to have been closed. But if one parent in the township insisted, it had to stay open. My father refused to agree to the closing, and my brother and I were sometimes the only students in the school; there were never more than five or six. That was a wise refusal.

We usually walked the mile to school, or rode two on a thin mule. We had two teachers there in eight years. Esther Kemen, calm and affectionate, had a boyfriend with a mustache and kept a pan of water on top of the coal stove in case we wanted to heat our cocoa for lunch, and a wire popcorn popper we could hold inside the stove and toast our cheese sandwiches. She had gone to this school, and her father also. For seventh and eighth grades, we had Marie Skulborstad, excitable and full of good energy. I kept a diary when I was eleven, and in the sixth grade, and I'll set down a few entries from it.

Jan 10.

Went to school. Took down some decoration. A new boy La Verne Shelstad. He is 14 years old and is in the 8th grade. My foot hurt so after school took boot off. Thinks my little toe has infection in between toes. Daddy and Mom went to a church meeting. Daddy was appointed delegate for church convention in June.

Jan 25.

Neither James nor I went to school on account of blizzard. I practiced my music lesson in grandma's room on Clara's piano. Got my magnifying glass from Post Toasties.

Jan 26.

Went to school. Walter and La Verne were there too. Got my 40 stamps from Grape Nuts Flakes. Got our report card from school. Couldn't go outside all day. La Verne couldn't either. Marie washed clothes.

Jan 27.

Went to school. Had spelling test sent out from Wroolie. I got 102. James 81, Walter 82, La Verne 82. My toe started to hurt again.

Feb 2.

Ground Hog day. Went to school. Got wet in school, walked home. Brought home book "Widow O'Callaghan's Boys." James brought home "Black Beauty." Walter got "Dark Frigate," and La Verne "Robinson Crusoe." Marie washed clothes.

Feb 3.

Went to school. Walked home. Played ping pong in school. Studied singing lessons. Finished reading book "Widow O'Callaghan's Boys." Art just came home today. His face was scratched.

Feb 13.

Went to Sunday School. Was going to Litchfield but was too icy. We got twin lambs from Western ewe. Daddy bought it from Julius Lund. We brought lambs into house. One was a buck and the other a ewe.

Feb 15.

Went to school. Got a letter from Grandma. Got whistling ring from Jack Armstrong. Marie washed and waxed floor. Snowed in night.

Feb 19.

Went to singing lessons. Found out I had to sing in musical. Have Key of D this time. Went over to Nelson's and shot a pigeon. Got package from Helma. It contained necktie and three handkerchiefs. Put sled together. Marie washed my head. Took bath.

Feb 20.

Went to Granma and Mervin's and Reuben's. I threw up just before we came to Willmar. Played Monopoly at Grandma's. Were going to Cities on Monday but Daddy decided not to.

Feb 21.

Went to school. Got six lambs. We have now 17 lambs. Mom, James and I went to show "Merrygoround of 1938."

Feb 23.

Went to school. Didn't get any lambs and none died. Mom had awful cold. Margaret Ehlenz died of double pneumonia just before 6:00 in the afternoon.

March 2.

Didn't go to school on account Teacher's dad was worse Cut off 22 lamb's tails which were upstairs. We couldn't cut off one lamb's tail upstairs. Worked on model planes. Fixed pen in chicken house for James' lambs and ewes and ones we raised on bottle. James has one old ewe and his old ewe. Mom and Daddy went to Roy's up at our old place. They moved a couple of days ago. Started reading "Hans Brinker and His Silver Skates."

March 3.

Went to school. Had Arithmetic, Geography and Spelling test. In Spelling I got 100, James got 94. In Arithmetic Test I got 94, James got 77. In Geography I got 92.

March 4.
Went to school. Had science test. I got 97. James got 95.

March 7.
Went to school. James got his Charlie McCarthy from Chase and Sanborn Coffee. It is just a cardboard. You can make his eyes and mouth move. Worked on plane. Got funny papers from Alvin. Had musical at Mrs. Smith's. I had to sing, "What Can I Give Him?" "Going Skating" and "While We Sleep."

March 23.
Went to school. La Verne wasn't there. James batted ball into ditch full of water, and it went into culvert. It lodged in middle of culvert. It got lost at last recess. Worked all last recess and till almost 4:15 after school. We still didn't get it out. Rode bikes.

March 24.
Went to school. La Verne did come. I brought fish pole and James a flash. Rode bikes. The fish pole was not long enough to reach ball. We sent in Walter's dog but it didn't do any good. Then we blocked up one end and washed it out. James took fish pole and flash home. I took lunchbuckets and my kite. La Verne had kite in school.

March 25.
Went to school. Had declamatory contest. I won in Humorous Readings. A Fudge girl was after me. In Dramatics a Fudge girl won. Also had spellings. Walter, La Verne, then James went down first. I was the 5th to last. I went down on Recipe. Name of my piece was Jimmie Jones Likes Geography. Worked on things in school. I stained 3 boards. Couldn't take bikes. I got haircut.

* * *

I grew up as a typical "boy-god." As I understand the idea, boys toward whom the mother directs a good deal of energy, either warm or cold, tend to become boy-gods. They are boys, and yet they feel somehow eternal, out of the stream of life, they float above it. My mother was and is a good mother, without envy or malice, affectionate, excitable, living with simplicity and energy—one of the servants of life. I had a brother a year and a half older, but I was the favorite son.

This embodied itself in a sense that I was "special," and so in a general lack of compassion for others. If someone were suffering, or in a rage, I would feel myself pull away, into some safe area, where I did not "descend" to those emotions, and get entangled in them, but neither did I help the person at all. What helping I did tended to be from above. We all know of people who bring Christmas gifts to the poor, or "help" old ladies by taking tea with them, who do not move others and are themselves unmoved. I was that sort.

The mood of Lutheran Sunday School only speeded up that tendency. It taught us that the body—that is, woman—was evil, and that purity lay in the eternal, in what was "up" . . . I already knew that. Rilke mentions the white dresses that girls wear at confirmation, but a woman will soon have to come down into her own body, certainly when she has a child she will. A man can remain floating for years, as I did.

In 1953, when I was twenty-six, I gathered into a little folder the poems that I had written to that time, almost every one the poem of a boy-god. Here is a poem I wrote when I was twenty-two.

You wonder why we take so many trips
And why our hours are all violent—
I speak of vegetation and the tide—
But when December storms the continent
And breaks the seas past any strength of ships
Now I remember Christ the crucified,
Who hurt his Mary, who could not help but say
At feast, "What have I to do with thee?"
Leaving for Jerusalem. This push
A baptist said was set in every knee
By that club-footed shape behind the bush
When life bent down to fire Adam's ribs.

There are peeling ferns inside Skid Row
Gospel missions in New Orleans
Where summer watched a woman put her hands

Around her husband, twenty years ago.
They spoke of love. He said, "Yes, forget it."
He left and walked to where he sleeps,
Where he eats his pork and beans from cans
And keeps a whore who has no teeth. These things
I heard. Learn them. They make some belief.
And I will leave you. That is another grief
That cannot be atoned in Copley Square
Body to body in the Christmas air.

In the Skid Row passage, when I referred to the experience there, it was not mine, but someone else's. That is typical of the boy-god. The cry "I will leave you" is the everlasting cry of the boy-god. He wants to be tied down to no one, especially not to a woman, and so he is always with "his hand on his lips, bidding farewell." The boy-god also typically explains the reason for his departure (which to him is the most exciting part of the love) as caused by vast, whirling forces, so cosmic that to obey is to be "pure," and so complicated in their working, that they could, of course, only be understood by "special people." The boy-god has a great sensitivity to the different resonances—which he interprets as dissonances—of the notes given off by spirit and body. The last line catches that perception of dissonance, in a tone which amounts almost to satisfaction.

The boy-god is often curiously cheerful—and I was cheerful almost all through childhood. This habit too becomes intensified in the Norwegian-American culture of the farms, where the social tone is a maddening cheerfulness, with no one ever admitting to being depressed or suicidal. No serious conflicts are ever found between separate areas of church doctrine, nor between capitalist practice and Christian practice. Only the oldest settlers, born in Norway, and socialists when they came, went around muttering in indignation at the latest news of corporate takeover. All deep conflicts of opinion are potentially depressing to one of the people arguing, if not to both.

In the middle of the Vietnam War, most people would limit themselves to "Well, we should never have gotten in there in the first place," a sentiment hard to build on. I was troubled all through my twenties by this insistent cheerfulness, and a little surprised at being troubled by it, since it had fit so well into the moods of high school. I finally realized it did not fit the moods of ancient civilization at all. I wrote this poem when I was twenty-four:

> When once astrologers read frozen stars,
> The stars said cold and death, and it was there.
> The blizzard of stars then shed remorseless snow
> Of terrible Novembers unborn yet,
> And earth was moving toward its death forever.
> We pore on men, and find the hoped-for June,
> And therefore to divine the mortal spring
> Deny the earth and contradict the stars;
> We, like musicians, read from written bars
> And ask musicians to be more true than stars.

It is still a boy-god's poem, with its obsession with stars and height. The poem notices that despite the love of stars, the boy-god, when pressed, will deny both the earth and the stars. He is just not sensitive enough to any heavy object outside himself. The movement toward secularization in recent history, the increasing emphasis on human beings instead of stars and "in-human" forces, and the movement away from a close life with nature, have both increased the power of the boy-god plague.

The poem also makes it clear that a symptom of the boy-god syndrome is his insistence—despite his conviction that he is special and thereby spontaneous and free—on reading music from written bars, that is to say, clinging to the safety of mind-concepts. Everything in the poem is mental. The mind-grids, developed over centuries in the seed, and over twelve years in the schools, interpose themselves between the boy and all sense experience. They "lift" him out of it. How high I was all through high school! What a terrible longing to come down!

* * *

And many hours shocking grain. That meant we went out in the morning with gloves, took two bundles of oats, and set them up on their butts, their foolish heads straying into each other. Then we found two more, and set those next to the first couple. Then we found two more for the far side. When these three pairs were in place, a mass of prickly oat spikes and itchy dust and smug straw, we put an outrider, or leaner, on each of the two sides, for good measure, making a total of eight bundles.

How many marriages we left in the field! And it was so beautiful to look back, and see all the houses standing in rows, not even rows either, but sometimes a shock poking out a little way this or that, and the ground all around cleaned of its burdens, naked, open to moonlight.

And I loved the nights after threshing, when the moon would hover over the strawpiles, all alone on some hill, far from the cluttered farmyards, with their itchy hens, stacks abandoned by the earthbound threshers whose horses obeyed them and took them home in the dusk. Sometimes I went back out into the fields, now so oddly silent—it was as if we went back to the Renaissance, where the fourteenth century lay in moonlight, only the people gone, the blood in all the marble—and sat on a new strawstack, looking at the moon, which was like a body just come from the bath, or the wheel of a bundle wagon everyone liked, or that round twist of hair at the back of a woman's neck.

* * *

We always had some suspicion of men from the town, who did not work with their hands. In town, they thought themselves better, but my father did not share that view, and he shielded us from its destructive radiation. He ran a threshing rig, and stood on it, respecting a number of grown men and even horses who worked with their hands, shoulders, and hooves all day. At times if we were threshing a field that the bank owned, having foreclosed during the late disastrous thirties—perhaps six or seven years before we were threshing—then the bank, to make sure the grain was divided properly, would send a cashier or teller out to watch the wagonboxes being pulled up to the thresher, and pulled away full, and where they went—from their cars—the bank often accepting their loads at a different elevator than the renter was using. How we pitied these creatures! Getting out of the car with a white shirt and a necktie, stepping over the stubble like a cat so as not to get too much chaff in his black oxfords, how weak and feeble! What a poor model of a human being! It was clear the teller was incapable of any boisterous joy, and was nothing but a small zoo animal of some sort that locked the doors on itself, pale from the reflected light off the zoo walls, light as salt in a shaker, clearly obsessed with money—you could see greed all over him. How ignoble! How sordid and ignoble! What ignobility!

* * *

A joy in growing up on a Minnesota farm at the time I did is that there was a place for men and women who could do only physical work. I knew mainly men of this sort, often bachelors. They never really knew that they were "dumb," because the farm culture was a hive that needed them. Their mother might mention to a neighbor in his hearing that the boy was "not cut out for school," but the tone of the sentence implied that a teacher was a curious kind of bird-trainer, whom one humored. They all knew that the real core of a boy lay in whether when sent out to the black fields he would go on working through the darkening light, whether he would get up in the middle of the night to check his ewes—for lambs born in midwinter can live only a few hours if they are not dried with a towel and taught to suck—or whether he could put on harnesses in the half-dark, still keeping the horse calm by not being irritable. These boys, when they grew up to be men, were usually patient with children, patient with cow dung and poorly lit barns, patient with slow horses and lodged barley. They could see they were needed. They hired out and lived forty or sometimes fifty years with the same family, at the start upstairs in a bare, unheated room, later perhaps in a small house or converted railway car, where they stayed snug through Sunday and never went to church. If you are needed, what does the rest matter?

Soon big machines began to appear, and we know what happened then. Only those with a fairly high IQ in the technical parts of the brain are allowed to farm. The reason for the spread of these large machines is not clear to me: historians usually mention shortage of labor. But there was no sign of that at all in the early forties, when they started to appear.

D. H. Lawrence, in his frightening essay "Men Must Work and Women As Well," says that one of the most important changes in the life of humanity had occurred during his own lifetime. That change amounted to the acceptance among all classes—he was speaking of England—of this idea: one should not do physical work. Other variations are, "We must go upward. Work with the head is higher than work with the hands." "Whoever is not fit to work in an office does not deserve respect." This idea appeared in China in Imperial times but was only accepted by the governing and scholar class. Here it is a secret sentence whispered in the four-minute gaps between high school classes, and through the walls of churches and government offices. It is especially whispered by stylish clothes and by the glazed fenders of the cars coming out of Detroit, where the models change every year: "We are angels, physical work is a mistake for us."

And what happens to the farm machines if physical work is bad? The early tractor, up to about 1950, was only a cast-iron engine with four wheels and a seat, made to pull heavy things, as clean in its way as a hammer or a spoon. First a simple cab was put on over the seat. Now the cab is luxurious, with a bucket seat, a dashboard that curiously resembles the communications panel of the executive's desk, side panels of imitation grained leather in black, tape decks for cartridge rock, and air conditioning. It seems to say, "All mental people deserve comfort."

The men who are not "cut out for school" now, when they reach eighteen, drift away into large cities, where they float like heavy steel washers enchanted by a medium, floating a foot or two below the ceiling of their small apartments. Others collect Social Security and sit with a television set, where they see the physical body killed again and again.

The unconscious does not hear well. It is a little deaf. It gets things wrong, because for two million years it has always done things its way and has only been talked to for the last three or four thousand years. If you say to it, "Physical work is bad," it may lose a word or two of that sentence. For some time it has been acting as if it heard, "Physical is bad."

Many college-educated people in their twenties and thirties are returning enthusiastically to work with their bodies, avoiding machines when possible. But on the farms no one has heard of the Whole Earth Catalog. Men in their twenties in western Minnesota getting into cars gesture with every motion their apology for having a body at all. In the living rooms of farmhouses one more and more often meets women without opinions. It is astounding, as my brother and I found out by throwing bundles of grain around twelve or fourteen hours a day, how much energy the body is capable of pouring out and then replenishing. That is a magical act, because you never really understand where all that energy comes from. Men and women who have experienced that are more likely to understand the idea that spiritual energy can also be poured out and replenished from mysterious sources. It is interesting to discover that those ecstasies involving high spiritual energy which we associate with the early Middle Ages in Europe continued well into the twentieth century in Tibet, a country so stark and cold the body has to pour out energy in amazing amounts simply to travel, or to stay warm, or to get food.

* * *

I'll tell you a story about my father. Each year men from south of us—Kansas, Missouri, Arkansas, even Alabama and Tennessee—would move through the country, following the small grain harvest north. They would end up in North Dakota or Canada about late September and would then go home again. My father, since he ran a threshing rig, would hire one or two of these men each threshing season. Sometimes I went with him, and at 6:00 A.M. before the rig had started, we would drive uptown to a small park in which some of the men had slept that night. If he saw a man with a face he liked, he would ask him if he could pitch bundles and drive a team or horses.

On one of those mornings, he hired a man whom I will call Garth Morrison, who had come up from a small town in Missouri. Garth turned out to be a good worker, and he and my father got on together very well. He stayed with us during the week. On Saturday night, the teams put away, he would go to town, and be gone Saturday night and Sunday night. But early Monday morning he would always be back and ready for work.

One Monday morning he didn't show up. My father was puzzled, and at about 9:00 A.M. he put someone else in charge of the rig and drove to town to see if he could find Garth. Asking around here and there, he heard that Garth had been picked up by the sheriff Saturday night. Apparently he had made a date with a waitress at a cafe, who had agreed to let him walk her home. At 11:00 he had gone to pick her up and, probably to his surprise, she did let him walk her home, where she lived with her parents. A few words were exchanged—probably a series of misunderstood signals between a southern man and a northern woman. He slapped her face. She went inside furious and complaining. Her parents called the sheriff. The man was from out of state. The sheriff and the judge had a secret court session the next morning—Sunday morning—having refused all along to let Garth call my father on the telephone, and sentenced him to twenty years at Stillwater prison. By Sunday noon he was on his way to Stillwater. By Sunday night the sheriff was back in town. It was said he always tried to show proof of his vigilance shortly before an election.

My father, once he got the story from the reluctant sheriff, was enraged. He shut down the threshing rig, and with his best friend, Alvin Hofstad, got in the car and drove to St. Paul to see the attorney general of Minnesota. The attorney general agreed that the facts gave off a bad odor. He went with my father and Alvin Hofstad to Stillwater, where they talked to Garth and verified the story. He then had Garth taken out of the prison and returned to the county jail in Madison to await trial. He stayed in the county jail a month or more, and we as boys would go up to talk with him through the window. My father hired a lawyer and paid for Garth's wife and son to come up from Missouri for the trial. They stayed with us and she testified at the trial; I remember her holding the baby on the stand. The jury convicted Garth of simple assault, and the judge ruled that the time already spent in jail more than served out the appropriate sentence. He was released and the family returned to Missouri.

My father never spoke to the sheriff again for the rest of the sheriff's life. Garth did not come north again either. The spring following the trial, Garth and his wife invited my father and mother down to Missouri for a visit. They drove down, and it turned out that everyone in that small Missouri town knew the story. When my father went for a haircut, the barber would not let him pay, and whenever he and mother went into a restaurant, the owner would not accept their money.

To be able to respect your father is such a beautiful thing! I learned then that the indignation of the solitary man is the stone pin that connects this world to the next. The more easy-going businessmen in Madison, who had so many friends, would have left Garth sitting in his cell for twenty years. They would have been afraid to put their hands into the web of social friendships, afraid the web would not be repaired overnight, or that the spider of loneliness would bite them. I learned too that when you have been unselfish, people respond not in words but by feeding you. I learned so much from that one story! We don't need to read books on ethics or to see documentaries on television; one moral example will do for a lifetime.

* * *

It is good to be alone near wood. I sometimes went to the top of the loft, where the hay was deep and a small high window looked out over the eastern fields. Up there someone had built a small shelf, just right to sit on. Its pale boards were miraculously strong so high in the air. I loved the knotholes, and the dusting of hay chaff in them, and in the corners and groins of the two-by-fours. Each one was a tiny intense house! Places looked at with such intensity on the day the barn was built and then never looked at again.

We had brought the hay in ourselves. Horses pulled the wagons right up and onto the second floor. Before throwing the first hay on the rack, we would lay down two ropes lengthwise on the rack floor; their ends, with snaps, hung down over the edges. When the hay was about to overflow the sideboards, we put down two more ropes on top of it for the second layer. Once the load of hay was in the barn, one of us would stand, his legs like a swimmer in deep water, rocking on top of the load, waiting for the lifters to be lowered from the track running way up in the skull of the barn. When they had come down, we snapped the rope ends of the top layer on and jumped off.

Then my father and perhaps Art below on the floor would pull on their long delicate rope, thick as a thumb, and slowly, with groans, the upper half, from the heart up, would begin to rise. What joy to see it lift, go up, farther and farther, into the dark top, darkness ascending into darkness, there was no end to its richness, the stomach sweaty and alive with dust, the body ready to run. Then the spreading of coarse salt, thrown in handfuls from a bucket—it salted the cows and the hay.

I wrote a poem with that barn in it later.

We are approaching sleep: the chestnut blossoms in the mind
Mingle with thoughts of pain
And the long roots of barley, bitterness
As of the oak roots staining the waters dark
In Louisiana, the wet streets soaked with rain
And sodden blossoms, out of this
We have come, a tunnel softly hurtling into darkness.

The storm is coming. The small farmhouse in Minnesota
Is hardly strong enough for the storm.
Darkness, darkness in grass, darkness in trees.
Even the water in wells trembles.
Bodies give off darkness, and chrysanthemums
Are dark, and horses, who are bearing great loads of hay

To the deep barns where the dark air is moving from corners.

Lincoln's statue, and the traffic. From the long past
Into the long present
A bird, forgotten in these pressures, warbling,
As the great wheel turns around, grinding
The living in water.
Washing, continual washing, in water now stained
With blossoms and rotting logs,
Cries, half-muffled, from beneath the earth, the living awakened at
last like the dead.

TIGERS AND HORSES

I'll say a few words about my life as a poet. I belong to a generation called the generation of 1962, along with Robert Creeley, Denise Levertov, Allen Ginsberg, Gary Snyder, Adrienne Rich, and John Ashbery. Our immediate teachers were well schooled in the poetry of England. English poetry is of high quality, but it is truly English poetry, not American poetry.

We were like animals who had been given a harness—the harness was the standard English poem, with its well-placed feet, the clattery sound of the horses' hooves, the black-painted carriage that it pulled behind, its sweet observances, its teas and proper ways. I could not stand it. I needed something else. It was in college that I found the first lines of William Blake, who said, "The tigers of wrath are wiser than the horses of instruction," and "The road of excess leads to the palace of wisdom." I decided not to go to graduate school; and so I put the horses of instruction out to pasture, and instead embarked on a garret life, which is in France the classic life of the young writer. I embarked on this life in New York.

Once one goes into that sort of life, it is difficult to come out. One has only a single pair of trousers, with patches, one begins to feel in oneself the sadness of the man who lives in a tiny room, knows no one important, and eats one meal a day. I lived a long time so, with no food, no publication, no support as a poet. Like a sinking ship, I fell a long way down through the layers of sea water, and came close to drowning.

> There is a joyful night in which we lose
> Everything, and drift
> Like a radish,
> Rising and falling, and the ocean
> At last throws us into the ocean.

At times my boat would come to the surface briefly. Then I lived like Noah, sending out a crow each day, and then when it returned, checking its feet to see if they had any mud on them. After two years of this life, a blessed thing happened. I walked along in New York, among thousands, and a man stopped me and asked, "Are you a poet?" No one could have given me a greater gift. He turned out to be an exiled Polish poet, hoping to find someone who could translate his poems. But he had picked me out of a hundred thousand, and made me feel that my secret was known, and I belonged to a long line of ignored young poets.

I'll call these years in the garret during my twenties the first stage of my writing life. In this first stage as a poet, I became a friend of loneliness. I made my living by painting houses one day a week. That was all right. If I hadn't achieved wisdom, I had at least been carried to my dark place by dragons or tigers, not by the horses of instruction.

I've described my early life as a writer. I expected to live my whole life that way, but it all changed. I married Carol Bly, and through a series of fortunate acts and rewards, I ended up in Norway, from which my ancestors had come almost exactly a hundred years before; and in Norway, thanks to a Fulbright grant, we had a stable life for a year, with an apartment, and a stipend. Now I had clothes: I could go to a respectable library; and it was in a library in Oslo that I read my first poem by Pablo Neruda. The first lines I read were:

> Young girls, with their hands over their hearts,
> Dreaming of pirates.

As I read more of his poems, I began to feel those floods of images that carry Neruda down like a great whale. Soon I discovered Cesar Vallejo as well, and I realized that the appropriate emotion for the 20th century is not religious ecstasy, nor cynicism, nor happiness, but grief. Neruda said:

> It so happens that I am sick of being a human being.

I learned that the only way to truly eat this grief, which is so nourishing, is through the image, the metaphor, the metaforo, the wild metaphor that escapes all bounds and leaps into the boat with us. I realized that the greatest poetry being written in the 20th century was in the Spanish language, in South America as well as in Seville and Granada and Madrid and Soria. In Granada, García Lorca was already playing his dark and stupendous guitar of *duende*—the same Lorca who greeted Pablo Neruda when he arrived from Rangoon in 1934. Still later I found the images of Miguel Hernandez, Blas de Otero, and many others. So it was the poetry in the Spanish language that saved me, and helped me escape from the English harness, and the English flatness. Spanish poetry fed me with the great and tremendous cries from the tigers of wrath and the dragons of sorrow.

It was Lorca with the images he created in his *Poet in New York* that helped us—as poets—to confront the Vietnam War when that time came in 1968, '69, '70, and '71. Lorca had said of New York:

> There is a wire stretched from the sphinx to the safety deposit box
> that passes through the heart of every poor child.

I founded with David Ray a group called American Writers Against the Vietnam War—other members were Lawrence Ferlinghetti, Galway Kinnell, Denise Levertov, Allen Ginsberg, Robert Lowell, and many more—and we gave during the war dozens—hundreds—of poetry readings to organize resistance against the war. It was a war connected to the safety deposit box, to colonial capitalism. Those images pioneered by Lorca, Neruda, Vallejo, and others helped us to write poems that were not merely expressions of anger, but expressions also of thought, grief, compassion, and fierceness—the "tigers of wrath." My own poem "The Teeth Mother Naked at Last" is an example of such work, a poem Ferlinghetti first published in his Pocket Poets series. This time was the second era of my writing life, when the loneliness lessened, and almost all the American poets gathered together, in a generous union, as friends and companions to combat the Vietnam War.

The First World War, in which 100,000 men died in one day, the Second World War, in which Russia alone lost 23 million people, the Holocaust of the Jews and Gypsies, the burning of the rain forests, the daily extinction of animal species, each of whom has as great a right to the planet as ourselves, the continuing cruelty to women, the steady decline of civility and courtesy everywhere, the fall in literary standards and education—how could our poetry not be sad?

I want to say to artists, don't be afraid to create social or political works of art. The best poems are not really "social"—they are about grief, in both women and men. Men are not suffering less than women. All that has helped for thousands of years to give dignity and meaning to men's lives—physical work, fatherhood, honorable labor, respect from their children—is passing away. Women are in as great a danger as men from computers, television, pop culture and global capitalism.

Perhaps I'm in the middle of a third stage of my writing life now. I won't describe it very far, because I'm still in it. But this stage has been blessed by the poetry traditions of the Islamic world. I translated some years ago poems of Rumi and more recently, with my son-in-law Sunil Dutta, who was born in Jaipur, the work of a nineteenth century Urdu poet named Ghalib. His poems are in the ghazal form, a term which indicated a love poem to the Arabs in the tenth century. Later the Persians and Hindus enlarged and adapted it, so it has become the main poetry form in the Islamic world. The classic ghazal has three characteristics. The first is that each stanza can have a different landscape—so one must leap a little while hearing or reading the poem. Secondly, the subject of the poem is never stated. That means more work for the reader to do. Thirdly, the same word is repeated as the final word in each stanza. Elsewhere in this booklet, a poem of mine called "Listening" has been included. For the moment, it can stand as an example of the ghazal as adapted into English.

LISTENING

The goose cries, and there is no way to save her.
So many cheeps come from the nest by the river.
If God doesn't listen, why are we listening?

Very deep water covers most of the globe.
Whenever I see it, I think of St. John.
There is no remedy for deep water but listening.

The King and Queen already know about love;
They search for each other through the whole deck.
While we play our hands, they are listening.

The day we die, we'll each be like the fish
Abruptly jerked out of the water.
For him, it is the end of all listening.

Like thousands of others, I'm eating beet soup
In some Russian inn. People write letters
To me from heaven, but I'm not listening.

The hermit said: "Because the world is mad,
The only way through the world is to learn
The arts and double the madness. Are you listening?"

WHEN LITERARY LIFE WAS STILL PILED UP IN A FEW PLACES

I first came to Iowa City in 1954, driving an old '42 Dodge which I had bought from a German exile in Boston for $65. I spent a couple of weeks on the way at the famous literary summer school in Bloomington, Indiana. John Crowe Ransom gave a talk on "A Litany in Time of Plague" by Thomas Nashe. One stanza reads:

> Beauty is but a flower
> Which wrinkles will devour;
> Brightness falls from the air,
> Queens have died young and fair,
> Dust hath closed Helen's eye.
> I am sick, I must die.
> Lord have mercy on us!

He noted that most teachers describe this poem as iambic, but if you speak the poem passionately, your voice will tell you the meter is not iambic at all. Powerful beats come in at the start of each line, so the meter is an imitation of the old Greek and Roman rhythms.

> Strength stoops unto the grave,
> Worms feed on Hector brave,
> Swords may not fight with fate,
> Earth still holds ope her gate.
> Come! come! the bells do cry.
> I am sick, I must die.
> Lord have mercy on us!

This marvelous lecture gave hints of new possibilities beyond the iambic mode I had been taught. I also saw William Empson with his long beard riding down the street on a bicycle. I mention these details only to give a sense of what high or elegant literary life was like in those days. It wasn't spread all over the country, so to speak, to a depth of one or two inches as it is now. Instead it piled up in separate places such as Gambier, Ohio, or Bloomington, Indiana, or even Iowa City, at a height of six or seven feet. I remember hearing that Robert Lowell, on his first honeymoon, pitched his tent on Allen Tate's lawn. He had a fine instinct for where the water was high. Jean Stafford later complained that he kept leaving her alone in the tent; he was always inside talking with the Tates.

When my $65 dollar car finally approached the center of Iowa City, I was astounded. The buildings were two stories high only. I guess I must have had in mind some sort of image as that I've just given, an image that associates literary intensity with physical heights, which may have translated itself into high buildings. I felt dismayed. I knew Robert Lowell had been teaching in Iowa City, and I said to myself, "What kind of country is this in which a poet that great is teaching in a town with two story buildings?" There's a lot wrong with my perception, but I was so self-centered and full of fantasies that there's not much use going into the inaccuracies. One could say that it wasn't as if Lowell had been exiled. Paul Engle, with his useful and intelligent impulse toward concentration of literary intensity, had called him there, and Lowell understood. Lowell's acceptance was a compliment to Paul's grasp of the way literature proceeds. A year or two later Engle brought in John Berryman; and Phil Levine's marvelous essay about Berryman's teaching in *The Bread of Time* suggests perfectly the way the physical presence of one superb writer, in this case Berryman, can change the life, and restructure the body cells, so to speak, of a younger writer ready to be made more intense.

I had come to Iowa hoping for a writing grant from the Rockefeller Foundation, but when I arrived, I heard it had gone to another, and so there I was in Iowa City with no money and no life. I went to see Paul Engle, and after some conversations with Ray West, and the head of freshman English, I was allowed to come into the workshop and given two classes to teach, one in freshman English and one called "Greeks and the Bible." The salary was $100 a month for each, as I recall, so there I was. I could get by on $200 a month, living in a tiny room and eating at a boarding house. Paul was generous, straightforward; he loved poetry, knew good poetry when he saw it, and was no slouch at building a program.

My only other workshop had been at Harvard with Archibald MacLeish. Among the participants were John Hawkes, Kenneth Koch, Don Hall, Mit Hughes, Bob Crichton, Bill Emerson. Most were World War II veterans, just now back in college, and all we did was attack Archibald MacLeish and belittle his friends such as Ezra Pound and Ernest Hemingway. We rarely discussed our own work. Our behavior was outrageous, and it took MacLeish a long time to get over it. So when I sat down in Paul Engle's workshop, it was the first time I had ever seen that strange thing, blue dittoed poems. I was amazed. It seemed beneath the dignity of art to mimeograph poems. We didn't attack the teacher this time; in general, the aggression went against each other. Everyone knew that W. D. Snodgrass, the graduate of an earlier workshop and still hovering in the neighborhood somewhere, had done something introspective and important in poems later called *Heart's Needle.* But he had to be careful if he turned up, because knives seemed to be out for him. That's the way I recall it. I don't recall being aggressive myself, but perhaps my memory is bad. I do remember hearing around 1975 a story of my behavior in the Iowa workshop twenty years earlier. It seems that I regularly brought a snake to class with me in a gunny sack, and whenever someone began to criticize a poem of mine, I would take the snake out and lay it on the table. I was amazed to be imagined as a snake handler. But we can feel several kinds of fear in this story

The workshop discussions were actually a little pedestrian; certain fads among the poets would dominate for a while. That's always the case with workshops. At the end Paul would come in and say rather sensible remarks. Given my history with MacLeish, whose lofty pronouncements floated down from some earlier heaven, this workshop was my first experience of literary democracy, even perhaps of that horizontal and envy-ridden culture which I later called sibling.

This piece will be more a memoir of the time than of Paul himself, but the literary excitement and dedication we all experienced was due to Paul's sagacity. The teaching most of us did made our lives rather hectic, and I commented in my diary, "In such a hectic life no large work can be conceived." I wrote in my diary one day, "I could work today only from 2:45, when I got back from a conference with Paul Engle, till 3:30, when I had to go to Muncie. Then I worked again from 5:30 to 5:45, hardly one hour altogether. I wrote the poem for Paul Engle, or rather attempted it. How wonderful it is to write poems for someone who cares about you!" So it was clear that I felt a lot of affection and support coming from him.

I also found notes from a conversation I had had with Paul, in which I remarked, "Paul's greatest need is precisely to be needed." So he and I were much alike in that way. He gave me advice on a group of poems I showed him, poems full of Ideas for poems and Possibilities for inner life. To me he always talked straight; he warned me about my grandiosity and my tendency to live six lives at once. His advice was very good: "Do one thing, not many." These were warnings that didn't do much good.

Many lively events happened in our workshops, and many able writers came to speak, but I failed to notice most of them. One personality did become vivid to me, a Korean short story writer, Kim Yong Ik, whom Paul had recruited for the fiction workshop. He and I would walk out in the Iowa City cemetery and look at the black-winged angel and talk about art. He looked at the creation of art as a marvelous opportunity which in the course of human life may arrive as a real possibility only once in every ninth or tenth generation. It had come to him. Dostoevsky was our hero, who would talk to himself in his room while he imagined some character in his fiction, and then he would weep over what had happened to that person. "Surely this is what writing really is—to give all," Kim said. And when we parted near dawn, he would say, "Tomorrow morning we must work very hard." He knew a lot. One day I brought to him a poem that I had begun in New York, and it said something like:

> I wander down the streets, not knowing
> Who I am, and I am lost.

Kim said, "Oh no. If you say you're lost, that means you're already partly found. If someone is in the woods and truly lost, he doesn't even know that he's lost."

I was stunned. "Well, what do I do then?"

"You just take out the phrase 'I am lost.' Then you compose some images that seem not to belong exactly, rationally. Then when the reader experiences those images, he will say, 'This kid is lost!' " I've been grateful for that for years.

He didn't believe in Western competition. Sometimes when we walked in the cemetery, he'd say, looking at the large stones and the small ones, "You see, even after death they're still competing." I asked him about Korean graveyards. He mentioned a graveyard with wooden markers in his town that stood on a slope. After a few years, the markers and graves would all wash down the slope. I must mention that Kim, who had lived for many years in Pittsburgh, writing well, died only a few months ago, during an emotional trip back to Korea.

I noted in my diary, "William Carlos Williams is coming next Monday." He read his poems in the old Capitol Building on campus. The head of the English department introduced him and said, "Tonight we have William Carlos Williams, one of the finest poets now writing in English." Williams stood up and said, "Goddam it! How many times do I have to tell you, I write in American, not in English!" That's what he was like. I loved him, and had hitchhiked to see him when I was an undergraduate.

Later in the spring, Robert Lowell came back for a visit, though he wasn't teaching at the workshop while I was there. I heard that he was staying at Ray West's house, so I sent a manuscript and, calling, asked if I could talk to him. He replied that he had to leave for the airport at such and such a time, but I could come. Here's how I described the fast glimpse of him in my journal: "He stood there hunched, a weight behind his eyes—gentle, graceful, unburning—wise in adaptation. How I trembled to meet him. How odd a poet is in this housey world, simply growing older among small things and small talk. What graceful hands draped questioningly at his chin . . . Marvelous is the word for him." I didn't describe our actual conversation in the diary. When I arrived, he was chatting with Ray West and Delmore Schwarz's first wife, getting ready to go to the airport. As they exchanged remarks, I was amazed to hear that the subject was William Carlos Williams, and his bad poems, ridiculous attitudes, his provincialism, etc. I began to burn. I knew that Williams had been and still was a sort of foster father to Lowell; Williams acted helpfully to balance the influence of Lowell's other, more conservative foster father, Allen Tate. Finally I spoke from my corner of the room, and said this wasn't a true picture of William Carlos Williams or his poetry. All three turned and looked at me as people look at a cockroach. They went on talking, but moved on to another subject. I waited further. Finally Lowell said, looking at his watch, "All right, come on over." He had in his hand the little manuscript I'd given him; he had picked out a brief poem that I had written the year before while living in New York and virtually as a hobo. After being cooped up in the city for months, I drove with friends in someone else's car down through Maryland and felt amazed by the great trees. The poem goes:

With pale women in Maryland,
Passing the proud and tragic pastures,
And stupefied with love

And the stupendous burdens of the foreign trees,
As all before us lived, dazed
With overabundant love in the reach of the Chesapeake,
Past the tobacco warehouse, through our dark lives
Like those before, we move to the death we love
With pale women in Maryland.

I was uncertain about the poem, uncertain about everything. What he said took me by surprise. He said, "Do you know which county you were passing through in Maryland?" "No," I said. "Well you could find that out," he said, "then go there; or go to a library and find out details of the history of that county. That's what I do," he said. "In that situation, I look up all the historical facts I can, find who founded that county, what sort of crimes took place, who introduced the tobacco farming, and so on. Then as I rewrite I try to get as many of those facts as I can into the poem." He wasn't unkind. At least his advice was clear. But I slumped out and was depressed for two or three weeks, saying to myself, "Well, that's it. If that's how a genuine poem is done, I can't do it. I'm not a poet." I didn't look at the poem again for a long time. Six years later, when I was gathering poems for what was at last to be my first book, *Silence in the Snowy Fields,* I found the poem again and realized that Lowell had been wrong. Some poems don't have historical facts, they just float. This particular poem is a bit elevated and naively romantic in its juvenile love of death, but still it has its integrity like a haiku or a small Chinese lyric. If one puts extraneous, interesting facts into such a poem, it will sink to the bottom of the river. I recalled a poem of Tu Fu's that Kim had often recited to me in Iowa City, a kind of exile's poem:

At the end of the mountain gorge
I hear dark monkeys wail,
In native land a white goose flies over.
Where are my sisters?
Where are my brothers?

This poem could use a few historical facts, perhaps, but if its aim is grief, it's best left as it is.

Paul and Mary would have big parties up at their stone house in Stone City, and I became fond of their children. In the spring of 1956, my wife Carol MacLean and I and Lew Harbison, a student of mine, and his wife went down to the Mississippi River bottoms a few miles south of Iowa City, all wet springiness and tall bare trees and flat ground recently abandoned by the river. High in a tree we saw two young great horned owls. Using a thin movable dead tree, we managed to push the owls along until they fell off the branch. Then we put them in a box and brought them back to Iowa City. I planned to bring the owls north to the Minnesota farm later that week. When Paul heard about the owls, he asked if I would bring them into his daughter's third grade class for the children to see. I did, and the little owls were spectacular, full of feistiness, with huge, intense eyes, like novelists or generals. A few days later, I did drive them up to the farm in Minnesota and let them go, and they were both around there in the draw for years, hooting to each other and wondering what happened to the Mississippi River flats.

When I heard in 1975 or so the story about the gunny sack I would take to class with the snake in it, I realized that it was the same story: the human proclivities for envy, projection and malice had altered the tale of two half-grown owls in a cardboard box in the third grade to a snake in a gunny sack in a graduate school classroom. So it is.

These adventures, these meetings with writers, this gathering place for people sick of small towns, all rose from Paul's sagacity. It was Paul who asked Marguerite Young, that amazing poet, essayist, raconteur, surrealist, fictionalist, to come to town. In my last dip into my diary, I'll put down a few sentences about her:

> Tonight I met Marguerite Young and once more the real world returns. Words, vision, meditation, the incredible greatness and sweetness of those on the limb of words. It is all words, and how the whole world dissolves away and leaves in its place the love for those people, and these people, who so love and in return are loved by words. Look into your heart; disregard the world of classes and deadlines and the blue world crossed with red, that entices and takes all away, that one cannot love. Love those who love words, and restrict your friendship to those.

"SNOWBANKS NORTH OF THE HOUSE"

William Stafford has spoken so beautifully about what an assertion means in a poem, and how early you can make one. In one of his books, maybe *Writing the Australian Crawl,* he says if you make strong assertions too early in the poem, you can lose the reader. The reader needs to receive a couple of assertions first that he or she can agree with, such as "It's summer," or "Animals own a fur world," or "Those lines on your palm, they can be read," or "There was a river under First and Main." The reader needs to experience rather mild assertions so that he or she can begin to trust your mind; then when you make a wilder assertion later, the reader is more likely to climb up with you into that intense place from which the assertion came. My first assertion is

Those great sweeps of snow that stop suddenly six feet from the house.

Some snow blows all the way down from Canada and then stops six feet from the house. For people who've never lived on the prairie and have experienced only gently falling snow or snow interrupted by woods, my first line may seem a risky assertion. So my second line is mild.

Thoughts that go so far.

I want my poem to continue, but not to ascend, so I need an ordinary event, something we've all known a thousand times:

The boy gets out of high school and reads no more books.

I can stay with that ordinariness for a little while:

The son stops calling home.

I experienced that refusal to call home when I lived in New York during my late twenties. Certain ways of living come to an end:

The mother puts down her rolling pin and makes no more bread.

I was thinking of my grandmother making Norwegian flat bread; readers correctly told me that ordinary bread these days is not made with rolling pins. But the child in me wrote that line. The adult in me wrote the next line:

> And the wife looks at her husband one night at a party, and loves
> him no more.

I'm not conscious that that line happened to me, but it's possible. I do recall seeing both halves of the line at one instant in the wife's glance. It's another sadness. It's just an ordinary sadness. It doesn't happen only to special people.

> The energy leaves the wine, and the minister falls leaving the church.

My father always had a particular tenderness for the old Lutheran minister in our town, and made sure that he received game such as pheasants in the fall, and geese at Christmas; I had some sympathy for the way a minister has to hold himself up and perform his role no matter what is happening in his private life. He has to keep giving the Communion.

A month or two after I wrote the poem, I read it to a friend who was an Episcopal priest of great spirit; he told me that I had described exactly what had happened to him a month before. He couldn't say the Communion words whole-heartedly on that particular Sunday, and he fell on the steps outside. One could say that for many ordinary people—and I am one of those—a fine energy sometimes refuses to become friends with us, or perhaps we refuse to make the courtly gesture that would welcome that energy. When we fall, it's an ordinary sadness.

> It will not come closer—
> the one inside moves back, and the hands touch nothing,
> and are safe.

I think a lot of my childhood is alive in that last half-sentence. And I spent in my mid-twenties two years alone in New York, talking to people barely once a month. It was all right. I felt safe: "The hands touch nothing, and are safe."

I must have felt that grief during the poem. The poem is moving away from sadness now and toward grief. And I recalled a scene from Abraham Lincoln's life. He loved his son Tad so much, and when the boy was eight, he died of tuberculosis or some such thing. They put the coffin into a room by itself in that kind of home visitation that people did at that time. Lincoln went into the room and didn't come out. He stayed all afternoon, and then he stayed there all night, and then he stayed there the next day. Around noon people started pounding on the door and telling him to come out, but he paid no attention. There was something a little extraordinary in that, but the general situation is not unusual, it's something we've all noticed or heard about many times. Sometimes after the death of a child, the husband and wife never do come back to each other.

> The father grieves for his son, and will not leave the room
> where the coffin stands.
> He turns away from his wife, and she sleeps alone.

Now what to do? Now we've arrived at a really ordinary place, in which life and its motions go on, but the shocked man or woman doesn't pay much informed attention to those motions anymore. Donald Hall has written about this place in his poem called "Mr. Wakeville on Interstate 90":

> I will work forty hours a week clerking at the paintstore. . . .
> I will watch my neighbors' daughters grow up, marry,
> raise children. The joints of my fingers will stiffen.

The way such a life moves mechanically is a form of depression. At the beginning of *A Farewell to Arms,* Hemingway says, "That fall the war was still there, but we didn't go to it anymore."

> And the sea lifts and falls all night, the moon goes on through the
> unattached heavens alone.

I loved that word "unattached" when I saw it on the page. It brought together the son who stops calling home and the man who lives alone in New York for two years.

Then I saw the toe of a black shoe. It seemed like an ordinary shoe, not standing on marble or red carpet, but on ordinary dust. Some elegant movement as of a hinge suddenly arrived, breaking all these long forward motions:

> The toe of the shoe pivots
> in the dust . . .
> and the man in the black coat turns, and goes back down the hill.

The first time I read the poem to an audience, there was some silence afterwards, and a woman asked, "Who is the man in the black coat?" I said, "I don't know." She said, "That's outrageous; you wrote the poem." I didn't answer. It was only when I got back to the farm that I thought of the proper answer: "If I had known who the man in the black coat was, I could have written an essay." I don't mean to demean essays with such a sentence, but it's good to think clearly in an essay, which can be a series of really clear and interlocking thoughts that are luminous. But sometimes a poem amounts to the creation of some sort of nourishing mud pond in which partly developed tadpoles can live for a while, and certain images can receive enough sustenance from the darkness around them to keep breathing without being forced into some early adulthood or job or retirement. It's possible the man in the black coat is Lincoln. He did turn and go back down the hill, and his face got sadder every year that the war went on. The other day I noticed in a family album a photograph of my father about 25 years old, standing by the windmill holding a baby rather awkwardly couched in his right arm; it's possible the baby was myself. He was wearing a large black coat. I don't know exactly why the last line closes the poem. I didn't intend it. It just came along. Perhaps it's the most ordinary thing of all. Our mother, or our grandmother, or grandfather, or our father, goes through incredible labors, keeping despite turbulent winds and strong blows the chosen direction forward, following some route. But why? What was the aim of Lincoln's life? What was the aim of my father's life? Or my life? We know a little bit of the story— what's the rest of the story? Why don't we know that?

> No one knows why he came, or why he turned away and did not
> climb the hill.

II.

VOCATION AND DISCIPLINES

THE VOCATION OF POETRY

It's my task tonight to say something sensible about the vocation of poetry. This is a hopeless task because many of us wander into poetry out of sheer love and only realize later that we're in a marriage. Thinking about the vocation of poetry, I've come upon ten labors and since I have only an hour, I'll have to do each labor in about five minutes. So to say that this lecture will lack depth is an understatement!

1.

I would say the first labor is to know the history of poetry in your own language. It won't do to say, "I'm just going to warble my native woodnotes wild." "I'm so original." The problem with that is that your sources are hidden to you, but not to us. There is no sense in repeating naively what others have said, simply by not knowing what they have actually said. It seems one needs to know what the earlier poets have done and then playfully add on to that.

2.

The vocation of poetry, particularly in Europe, involves knowing not only the poetry in your own language, but in other languages. One sees that very clearly in the lives of Polish poets, of Czechoslovakian poets, of Swedish poets. For many poets in Europe, it's as if the poets all over Europe are aiming at a single group of poems, poems of a certain flavor and personality, even though written in different countries. Rainer Maria Rilke for example not only studied poetry in French but actually wrote an unusual number of poems in French. One feels in Whitman that sort of generous attitude toward poets of other lands. He often addresses them, and points out that they're working on a similar project together. Many of the greatest poets we have had in the United States during this century have also been enthusiastic translators. T. S. Eliot translated Saint John Perse and La Forgue. Eliot's poetry is unthinkable without the earlier writing of La Forgue. Kenneth Rexroth translated Japanese and Chinese poets. Pound is a famous example of an American poet who stepped far outside the boundaries of poetry in English and definitely considered that a part of his vocation as a poet. Closer to our time, Robert Lowell made many highly inaccurate translations, and Richard Wilbur exquisitely faithful translations of Moliere.

3.

The vocation of poetry in the past often meant that you agreed to be a musician. We know that Alcaeus's and Sappho's poems were always sung. They were written in a specific meter so that they would all fit to a tune. Shakespeare's sonnets were definitely sung. The word "sonnet" is related to the word "sonata." A famous poem, "Drink to Me Only with Thine Eyes," still retains its tune in our memory. Blake's poems were all set to music. All the settings are lost. As we know, in Persia Hafez and Rumi were sung. My wife and I were once in London at a performance of Persian poetry, and after two hours of singing the Iranian audience began to shout up the names of tunes and therefore poems of Hafez and Rumi that had not yet been sung that night. All of those tunes have been preserved. I'll give you an example of a Hafez poem:

> Let's take the yellow flowers and throw them all around.
> Let's pour some wine, the best that can be found.
> Let's smash the bowl of the great heavens
> And start the creation over again.

4.

Poets have always been expected to know the mystery of the Seven Holy Vowels. We have a book of that name written by Joscelyn Godwin. I brought along several of these books so you could see them. The particular vowels that are considered holy are the open vowels, which vary somewhat in every particular language. But roughly we could say that they are

EE / AI / AH / AY / OOH / EH / and OH

In the work of knowledgeable poets, a stanza will be dominated by two or three or these vowels, which reverberate against each other and give a firm oral beauty to the lines or stanzas. The long vowels have the sensation of giving the stanzas weight. The most famous of the poems written in recent times using such vowels is Yeats's "Lake Isle of Innisfree." I'll recite it here so you can hear these vowels.

> I will arise and go now, and go to Innisfree,
> And a small cabin build there, of clay and wattles made:
> Nine bean-rows will I have there, a hive for the honeybee,
> And live alone in the bee-loud glade.
>
> And I shall have some peace there, for peace comes dropping slow,
> Dropping from the veils of the morning to where the cricket sings;
> There midnight's all a glimmer, and noon a purple glow,
> And evening full of the linnet's wings.
>
> I will arise and go now, for always night and day
> I hear lake water lapping with low sounds by the shore;
> While I stand on the roadway, or on the pavements grey,
> I hear it in the deep heart's core.

5.

In ancient times, the vocation of the poet also included knowing how to recite. That quality is not as pronounced now, and many poets find it more humble to mumble their poems, or it has never occurred to them that it's necessary to carry the poems all the way to the audience. I remember the first poetry reading I gave in my life, which was to a group of Americans in Oslo in 1958. I was already 32 years old, but I knew nothing of that part of the vocation of poetry. I was fairly near the audience on the same level, and I saw my words go out a few feet from my mouth and then fall to the floor before they reached them. I remember remaining awake half the night over shame of that. So when you're reciting poems, it's your job to carry the lines and the sounds over to the audience. Pablo Neruda was an amazing example of that. We had a celebration for his hundredth birthday in Washington last week and we saw a five-minute clip of him reading and talking. The poems all came out in a sort of mournful tune. It was as if a man were talking who had lost his wife or mother. He was like an old mother on the steps of a church, mourning the death of her son. But the poem no matter the content always came through. In the little clip he told a lovely story of having his plane come down because of bad weather in a relatively small Chilean town. When the people in town realized he was there, they asked for a reading that night. He agreed and began to recite the Poem number 20 in his book of poems *Twenty Poems of Love and One Ode of Desperation.* He began the poem, "I think I could write the saddest lines tonight." Then his memory failed him. The audience realized it; without missing a beat, they recited back to him the entire rest of the poem. So in the clip he said, "So I was the only person in Cartagena who had not memorized Poem number 20."

6.

To be a poet means to occupy the position of the wise woman or wise man of your tribe. That is responsibility, and it does not belong to a nation or to a huge community; it really belongs to a tribe. There was the shaman and there was the leader and there was the poet; and all three of those are positions that require some wisdom. One of our greatest examples is Emily Dickinson, who was constantly saying wise things to the little tribe there in Amherst. And why should she publish her poems in national magazines? Wyoming is not a part of her tribe. If we were to choose a man who understood this, one example would be William Blake. He knew he belonged to a tribe of eccentric empire-hating, God-loving radicals who made up a relatively small tribe in England. But great people were in that tribe. He has some wisdom to say about London where his tribe lived:

> I wander through each chartered street
> Near where the chartered Thames does flow
> And mark in every face I meet
> Marks of weakness, marks of woe.

He's saying the opposite of what he hears in the newspapers and most of the sermons.

> In every cry of every man,
> In every infant's cry of fear,
> In every voice, in every ban,
> The mind-forged manacles I hear.

So he's warning the tribe that the oppression is coming not from some other country but from our own mind.

> How the chimney sweeper's cry
> Every blackening church appalls
> And the hapless soldier's sigh
> Runs in blood down palace walls.
>
> But most through midnight streets I hear
> How the youthful harlot's curse
> Blasts the newborn infant's tear
> And blights with plagues the marriage hearse.

As you know, the authorities, to lessen the danger of revolt, were selling bottles of gin for one or two cents each. He warns the tribe that it's getting sick. He gave some other thoughts to his tribe in the famous "Proverbs of Hell," for example:

> The road of excess leads to the palace of wisdom.
>
> He who desires but acts not breeds pestilence.
>
> If the fool would persist in his folly, he would become wise.
>
> Exuberance is beauty.
>
> As the caterpillar chooses the fairest leaves to lay her eggs on, so the priest lays his curse on the fairest joys.

A poet has some obligation to offer what wisdom he or she has for his tribe. It's the poet's job to be helpful to people living at his or her time. T. S. Eliot says things like "Do not ask for more. We have our inheritance."

7.

From the obligation the poet has to offer some wisdom to his or her tribe, we could also say that when the tribe becomes a nation, the poet can be expected to present a political point of view. We know how vital and important Voznesensky and Yevtushenko were to the nation of Russia. We remember Robinson Jeffers's opposition to the plans for World War II. William Stafford advised all the men his age to do conscientious objection, and he spent two years in a CO camp as a punishment for that.

> I was a prisoner
> Someone brought me gifts. . .
> In camps like that, if I should go again,
> I'd still study the gospel and play the accordion.

The massive number of poetry readings that we had in this country against the Vietnam War made clear for years that the poets were accepting this part of the vocation of being a poet. Robert Lowell led the march against the Pentagon. Robert Duncan, Allen Ginsberg, Galway Kinnell, and Denise Levertov all took a strong part through their poetry in the protests. All of us were following Whitman, who said,

> Why reclining, interrogating? why myself and all drowsing?
> What deepening twilight—scum floating atop the waters,
> Who are they as bats and night-dogs askant in the capitol?
> What a filthy Presidentiad! (Oh South, your torrid suns! Oh North, your arctic freezings!)
> Are those really Congressmen? Are those the great Judges? Is that the President?
> Then I will sleep awhile yet, for I see that these States sleep, for reasons;
> (With gathering murk, with muttering thunder and lambent shoots, we all duly awake,
> South, North, East, West, inland and seaboard, we will surely awake.)

Because I think this vocation of the poet is particularly important, and we seem to have less of it during this war, I've written a book called The *Insanity of Empire: A Book of Poems Against the Iraq War,* which is just being published now. It will be out in two weeks or so. If you want to leave ten dollars and your address up here at the desk, we'll make sure that you're mailed a copy of that book as soon as it's out.

8.

There are other promises embedded in the vocation of being a poet, and I think one is that you agree to keep communication open — to what? — I would say to nature. Everyone recognizes that Whitman made some amazing step after the 18th century had finished. In that century, the ideas and the life of the mind preoccupied Dryden as well as Alexander Pope and Swift. Wordsworth reopened the communication with nature in such a wholesale way that he was mocked by the literary community for years.

My heart leaps up when I behold
a rainbow in the sky. . . .

I wandered lonely as a cloud
That floats on high o'er vales and hills,
When all at once I saw a crowd,
A host, of golden daffodils;
Beside the lake, beneath the trees,
Fluttering and dancing in the breeze.

Continuous as the stars that shine
And twinkle on the Milky Way,
They stretched in never-ending line
Along the margin of a bay:
Ten thousand saw I at a glance,
Tossing their heads in spritely dance.

When I was growing up in western Minnesota on a farm, that communion with nature felt to me to be the exact place at which to begin a life of poetry. My first book was called *Silence in the Snowy Fields,* and I'll read you the poem that has stuck in my mind since that time.

I
Oh, on an early morning, I think I shall live forever!
I am wrapped in my joyful flesh,
As the grass is wrapped in its clouds of green.

II
Rising from a bed, where I dreamt
Of long rides past castles and hot coals,
The sun lies happily on my knees;
I have suffered and survived the night
Bathed in dark water, like any blade of grass.

III
The strong leaves of the box-elder tree,
Plunging in the wind, call us to disappear
Into the wilds of the universe,
Where we shall sit at the foot of a plant,
And live forever, like the dust.

This opening toward nature, adopting that as one of the tasks of being a poet, seems to be more important than it has ever been. When work is over these days, men and women are not taking walks. Most of them are not working in their garden. They are in the basement communing with the fourth-rate minds of the television bureaucrats. It's really much worse than the 18th century concentration on reason, because the reasoning was done with other people. Now the citizen is alone, isolated, returned to adolescent anxiety.

9.

The vocation of poetry has always implied that you will be in some way an open spokesman for joy. Perhaps the *Song of Songs* comes to mind. In Yeats's book called *The Winding Stair*, published when he was 68 years old, he brings in this duty to speak of joy as the dominant demand in the book. He talks about the absence of it in three lines:

Shakespearian fish swam the sea, far away from land;
Romantic fish swam in nets, coming to the hand;
What are all those fish that lie gasping on the strand?

He says:

I am content to follow to its source

Every event in action or in thought;
Measure the lot; forgive myself the lot!
When such as I cast out remorse
So great a sweetness flows into the breast
We must laugh and we must sing,
We are blest by everything,
Everything we look upon is blest.

He had the sense that part of the joy of nature is that mist and snow are a little bit mad. And the old poets were a little bit mad, too, compared to us. So he said:

Bolt and bar the shutter,
For the foul winds blow:
Our minds are at their best this night,
And I seem to know
That everything outside us is
Mad as the mist and snow.

Horace there by Homer stands,
Plato stands below,
And here is Tully's open page.
How many years ago
Were you and I unlettered lads
Mad as the mist and snow?

You ask what makes me sigh, old friend,
What makes me shudder so?
I shudder and I sigh to think
That even Cicero
And many-minded Homer were
Mad as the mist and snow.

We notice that many young people are trying to learn the vocation of poetry through university MFA programs, and hundreds of poets are being baptized each year and given their rights as poets upon completion of the courses. And yet, we see very little madness in these poems. Perhaps I wouldn't recommend trying to be both a poet and an English teacher, because both of them are vocations, and very important ones. I'm not sure that one can sustain both in one lifetime. I remember that when I was an undergraduate, Richard Wilbur said to me and a couple of others, "I realize that I cannot be a good poet and a good teacher both. So I've decided to be a good poet and a bad teacher." For him that seems to have worked out well; he's still writing well. The clarity of his mind about that is very beautiful.

10.

The tenth task in the vocation of being a poet many of you will find even more distasteful than some of the early ones The old vocation of being a poet meant that the poet would keep up his or her connection with the divine. Again, Emily Dickinson put that first in her many obligations. You remember her poem:

> Exultation is the going
> Of an inland soul to sea,
> Past the houses — past the headlands —
> Into deep Eternity —
>
> Bred as we, among the mountains,
> Can the sailor understand
> The divine intoxication
> Of the first league out from land?

So for her, the sea and the divine are one. The secular and the land are one. Gerard Manley Hopkins is superb in this area of the poet's vocation. He said:

> I have desired to go
> Where spring not fail,
> To fields where flies no sharp and sided hail
> And a few lilies blow.
>
> And I have asked to be
> Where no storms come,

Where the green swell is in the havens dumb,
And out of the swing of the sea.

We all know his poem, "God's Grandeur."

The world is charged with the grandeur of God.
It will flame out, like shining from shook foil;
It gathers to a greatness, like the ooze of oil
Crushed. . . .

And at the end of the poem, he says:

Because the Holy Ghost over the bent
World broods with warm breast and with ah! bright wings.

I have told you enough now of what I feel is implied when one agrees to take up that old burden and joy of living a life of poetry. Perhaps I've given too many qualities or not enough. Looking at it another way, one could say that the vocation of poetry does not imply that you will tell everyone what is wrong with your parents. That's a recent addition to the list. It doesn't imply either that you will keep your concentration on any one class of people, either the rich or the poor. It doesn't imply that you will have to be a good person—it appears that the French were perfectly right to hang Francois Villon.

In the Muslim world, the vocation of a poet implies that you will be a lover of the Divine Face. We had that for a few decades with the Troubadours in southern France. But in the Muslim world, the poet's love for the Divine Face is the distinguishing mark of all his poems. We can see it in Rumi and Hafez:

No one has seen your face, and yet a thousand
Doorkeepers have been appointed.
You are a closed rose,
Yet a hundred nightingales have arrived.

We all know some of the lovely stanzas of Rumi that Coleman Barks has translated:

"I would like to kiss you."
"The price of kissing is your life."
Now my loving is running towards my life shouting,
"What a bargain! Let's take it!"

So this is the end of our little excursion into the vocation of a poet, and if you have noticed some obligations or possibilities that I have forgotten, please mention them to me. I'd like to hear your opinions on this terrifically interesting subject.

2004

SIX DISCIPLINES THAT INTENSIFY POETRY

One could think of twenty skills or practices or disciplines that may help good writing turn into poetry. I've chosen these six out of many possibilities. Every veteran of the wars might choose a different six. The first I'll mention is the Delight of Metaphor.

We always have a choice between facts—I broke my knee when I was five, I have always been bad at math—and metaphor. A metaphor resembles a storm—it is a God-given gift to the countryside, it is a form of intensity like dancing; a good metaphor breaks open the stagnant mind and makes available the other mind's storehouse of raisins, macaroons, and jewels. When Pablo Neruda begins "Ode to My Socks," he opens with a couple of facts:

> Maru Mori brought me
> a pair
> of socks
> which she knitted herself
> with her sheepherder's hands. . . .

That's enough facts, and now he turns to metaphor:

> I slipped my feet
> into them
> as though into
> two
> cases
> knitted
> with threads of
> twilight
> and goatskin.
> Violent socks,
> my feet were
> two fish made
> of wool,
> two long sharks

sea-blue, shot
through
by one golden thread,
two immense blackbirds,
two cannons:
my feet
were honored
in this way
by
these
heavenly
socks.

What blessings does metaphor give? It prevents the mind—the uneducated or the educated mind—from going straight ahead down a railway of slumbering, half-interesting facts. Instead the metaphor stops the train, tells all the literalists to get out. Finally they can see some open fields.

I slipped my feet
into them
as though into
two
cases
knitted
with threads of
twilight
and goatskin.

The metaphors open doors to weather, to knitting, to animals, to nature. The writer who insists on metaphor carries us out of our room, into the forest, where, Lorca says, all poems are found. Lorca remarked: "When I sit down, I always write with green ink, so that I don't frighten the wild animals. Gerardo Diego claims that he uses red ink, but we all know that he lies about things like that." Lorca begins "Little Infinite Poem" this way:

To take the wrong road
Is to arrive at the snow

And to arrive at the snow
Is to get down on all fours for twenty centuries and eat the grasses
    of the cemeteries.

Whether we can use metaphor with the swiftness and purity of the masters is not the point; even playfully climbing on metaphor, riding that horse, brings us into the kingdom of uncertainty, where a mouse can come along wearing King George's hat. Of course, we all know that simply using metaphors will not make the poem good in itself; the metaphors have to be fine.

A few years ago Don Hall and I gave a reading of our worst poems; we tried to trump each other and see who had written the worst poem. I offered this early poem.

The green poet goes through the world
Riding on the bark of a tree.

He walks in the city streets meditating
Like the fleece of a sheep.

Or climbs on trains and buses
With a tree growing from the sole of his foot.

Alone at last he sits in his room,
His face surrounded by leaves.

And he carries inside
Six tiny grains of mustard seed

And the seeds of wild strawberries,
And in his shirt the loaf of bread

Baked on the stormy day
When the Roman Empire ended at last.

The idea that sheep's wool does meditation is a doubtful proposition. I especially enjoy the idea of the writer climbing on a bus with a tree growing from the sole of his foot, which seems very cumbersome.

The genuine metaphor wakes the reader up abruptly. D. H. Lawrence in his tortoise-shell poem says:

> I remember my first time hearing the howl of the weird amorous
> cats;
> I remember the scream of a terrified, injured horse, the
> sheet-lightning,
> And running away from the sound of a woman in labor, something
> like an owl whooing. . . .

The metaphor often opens the soul to the nonhuman world. Mary Oliver's "Sleeping in the Forest" goes this way:

> I thought the earth
> remembered me, she
> took me back so tenderly, arranging
> her dark skirts, her pockets
> full of lichens and seeds. I slept
> as never before, a stone
> on the riverbed, nothing
> between me and the white fire of the stars
> but my thoughts, and they floated
> light as moths among the branches
> of the perfect trees. All night
> I heard the small kingdoms breathing
> around me, the insects, and the birds
> who do their work in the darkness. All night
> I rose and fell, as if in water, grappling
> with a luminous doom. By morning
> I had vanished at least a dozen times
> into something better.

The poet, Jay Leeming, who hasn't published his first book yet, showed me a new poem of his the other day. His metaphors don't necessarily open you to nature, but they do something very swiftly.

Trying to get rid of your ego
Is like trying to get rid of your garbage can.
No one believes you are serious.
The more you shout at the garbage man
The more your neighbors remember your name.

Here the metaphor does operations swiftly that it would take a Buddhist prose speaker hours to do.

Ananda Coomaraswami said something like: "To have lost the art of speaking in images is precisely to have lost the ability to touch the world of spirit and to have descended instead into the dry planes of philosophy."

Hart Crane said about Labrador:

A land of leaning ice
Hugged by plaster-grey arches of sky
Flings itself silently
Into eternity.

Hart Crane's "Voyages II" ends this way:

Bind us in time, O seasons clear, and awe.
O minstrel galleons of Carib fire,
Bequeath us to no earthly shore until
Is answered in the vortex of our grave
The seal's wide spindrift gaze toward paradise.

The seal's "wide spindrift gaze toward paradise" reveals the deepest longing and the most ferocious secret of metaphor, namely that it can shift us, as no other gift can, to the plane of the divine, to the rooms of Paradise, to the roof beams of heaven.

THE ANCIENT FRIENDSHIPS BETWEEN SOUNDS

When we sit down to write, we often imagine that thoughts are coming, or feelings are arriving. But actually what are arriving are syllables, each a marriage or affair of vowel and consonant. As we write along at our desk, we watch sometimes with amazement these little sound units or particular love affairs coming along in their variety. They keep coming along, no matter what we do.

But it is another thing to take part in their arriving—to put out a call for sound friendships, to decide to encourage certain ones. Then we are awake by one more degree. To be awake as a writer is to take part in sound friendships and welcome them.

Let's take a small poem and look at it, keeping the repeating sounds in mind. This is a poem by Robert Creeley.

> Love comes quietly,
> finally, drops
> around me, on me,
> in the old ways.
>
> What did I know
> thinking myself
> able to go
> alone all the way.

The word "quietly" introduces the "ai" sound, and adds to it with "finally." "Quietly" also introduces an "ee" sound, which reappears twice as "me." But we also notice a few affairs that vowels have with "n"—"finally," "around," "on." With the word "old," something begins to shift, and the vowel "oh" begins to push its way in, dancing a bit with the earlier "ai" sound.

> What did I know
> thinking myself
> able to go
> alone all the way.

"Thinking" and "alone" honor the consonant "n"; and halfway through the stanza "ay" begins to enjoy itself. Nature loves repetition; and we could say that the little poem of Robert Creeley's has become an imperishable object of nature while pretending only to be art.

These tiny particles of spoken sound which are announced on paper as *in*, and *ar*, and *or* and *an* and *un* are lovely things! The language experts, who have very little sense of language, call them phonemes. Please forget that right away. Calling them sound particles is OK for now. Grasping these little sounds with the pincers of our ears is the most exciting process we can learn to do—it is like the study of Egyptian artifacts. They are really little creatures—*in* and *am* and *el* and *il* and *en*. A sound friendship, or a sound-urn contains the delicate, easily destroyed artifacts of music. A sound particle or being is the union of a heavily veiled vowel and a consonant, the one leaning on the other, so to speak, two friends who are never parted, who always sing the same little tune, no matter how it's spelled.

I've counted about eighty of these sound particles, or sound creatures, or sound friendships, in current spoken English. As we know if we have listened to Coleman Barks, strange sound particles flow out of the mouths of people in the Deep South, involving vowels that never pass New England lips. So we shouldn't be too Germanic and picky about how many sound particles there are in the many variations of the English language. One of the reasons I fell in love with *Lord Weary's Castle* when I was in college was because Lowell's ear is so receptive to *ar* and *in*. There's a great deal of pleasure in *Lord Weary's Castle*, which is really also the pleasure of sound. Here are the first five lines of "The Holy Innocents":

> Listen, the hay-bells tinkle as the cart
> Wavers on rubber tires along the tar
> And cindered ice below the burlap mill
> And ale-wife run. The oxen drool and start
> In wonder at the fenders of a car . . . .

You can see he's stretching things a little here and there in order to get "car," "cart," "tar," and "start" in succeeding lines, but that's what a musician does. He also brings in several *urs* and *ires*. He also honors the affairs *n* has with its lovers: uncle, cindered, run, oxen, wonder, fender. Finally it all seems right, or nearly right, because we are being fed at some deep level.

Let's give one more example of the way we can grasp these tiny sound particles with the pincers of our ears. Elsewhere in this issue we reprint Jane Hirshfield's "The Envoy." She is talking of a rat and a snake who entered her room one winter. She associates them with "something" that entered her body that year.

> Not knowing how it came in,
> not knowing how it went out.
>
> It hung where words could not reach it.
> It slept where light could not go.
> Its scent was neither snake nor rat,
> neither sensualist nor ascetic.
>
> There are openings in our lives
> of which we know nothing.
>
> Through them
> the belled herds travel at will,
> long-legged and thirsty, covered with foreign dust.

The word "openings" is good. Those belled herds, travelling "at will," are superb side-steppings of the literal, and she offers the joy of metaphor.

Yet we notice that the metaphors retain some cunning power because she has paid careful attention to what we have called sound friendships, the friendships of vowel and consonant.

> Its scent was neither snake nor rat

Notice the *en* and the *nye* and the *snay.*

> Its scent was neither snake nor rat.

And now, while staying with *sen,* she adds *ist* and *as*:

> neither sensualist nor ascetic.

We can see why people who write poetry are traditionally associated with lovers. Who but a lover could honor these friendships of the shy vowel and the often ignored consonant. One would have to be—to love these friendships well—neither sensualist nor ascetic.

Marvell is a genius in sound friendships:

Yet happy they whom grief doth bless
That weep the more, and see the less:
And to preserve their sight more true
Bathe still their eyes in their own dew.

We notice first the *ear* and *air*, or *or* music—"preserve" comes forward, and merges toward "their" (three times), and "more" (two times). And we notice the *ay* sound—"happy they"—merging with "Bathes." "Weep," "grief," and "see" make a sound trio, and of course, encouraged by the rhyme, "true" and "dew," "bless" and "less." The old rhyme schemes did at least alert the writer to gain at least two resonances in a stanza, like an engagement party and a wedding that leads us to chose at least two gifts.

Thus sung they, in the English boat,
An holy and a cheerful note,
And, all the way, to guide their chime
With falling oars they kept the time.

He is one of the few poets who lifts the *and* at the start of a line in such a way that in this poem it chimes nicely with "sung" and "an" and "English." *Ay* is chosen. And he lifts the *oh* sound up beautifully, with "boat" and "holy" and "note." There are many other chimings here we don't need to point out.

Perhaps we've said enough about sound particles. A skilled reader can tell instantly—within a half-line or so—whether the poet is conscious of this discipline, or just writing along, like a dog or cat going down the street. W. B. Yeats always emphasizes that, for the heart to take in a poem, the soul in us has to go into a slight trance; and that can't be done by assertion, nor image, for fact, nor meter. The music of the sound particles induces the trance. We can feel it deeply in "The Lake Isle of Innisfree."

Having mentioned "The Lake Isle of Innisfree," we might say a few words about what are called the long vowels. When it is "long," the sound itself is so strong, so penetrating, that it seemingly exists without any partners, somewhat the way Queen Elizabeth reigned in court with no visible paramours.

In much ancient poetry, the main kinetic energies of the line, its feet, so to speak, rest in the long vowels. If you hear a Farsi speaker reciting Rumi or Hafez today, you find yourself swimming in a sea of long vowels, and the shorter vowels and their consonant companions are like little rafts. Attention to long vowels leads directly to dance. Pindar's poems were danced. Later both Sappho and Alcaeus developed more intricate dances, patterns of long and short vowels that were so satisfying that poets used them for centuries. As I mentioned, Tranströmer used them in 1962.

How many long vowels are there—those Queenly and Kingly vowels? Traditionally, seven. The seven we'll discuss here are *ay* as in "hay," *ee* as in "sea," *oh* as in "holy," *oo* as in "you," *ai* as in "tiny," *ah* as in "father," and *ohm* as in "home." It's possible that we have been responding physically to these vowels since we were in the womb. *The Secret Life of the Unborn Child* by Thomas Verny, for example, provides evidence, some gained by ultrasound experiments, that babies in the womb make motions that correspond to each of the long vowels.

Donald Hall, in his brilliant essay "Goatfoot Milktongue Twinbird," relates the joys of sound to mouth pleasure of the infant after birth. He calls the shameless enjoyment of vowels (which Dylan Thomas did so well) "milktongue," as if our love of poetry began while nursing, as if we remember the sensual joy at the nipple well into adult life. If the poet doesn't open his or her mouth wide enough at poetry readings, Don will accuse him or her of "mouth-guilt." Several times he has accused me of this fault, which is not really a fault, but a simple characteristic of Midwestern farmers. It's clear from reading Dylan Thomas that he was a big nipple man. I'm afraid were getting distracted here.

We won't spend a long time going over each vowel, but we might mention that some ancient gods had names made only of vowels. There was the old Mediterranean god Iao, which in our phonetic system probably would sound like *Ai-ah-oh.* The long vowel *ai* corresponds anciently to the sun. As for *ah* and *oh,* they are alpha and omega, the first and last letters of the Greek alphabet—so the name Iao could mean then Divine Sun Energy that Begins and Ends All Things. In many cultures *ah* is felt to be the strongest vowel of them all. We notice it appears once in our word "God," but twice in the Muslim word "Allah."

Goethe knew all of these ideas, as we can see from applying his knowledge to the poem "Wanderers Nachtlied II," or "The Second Song the Night Walker Wrote." He chooses the moment the sun begins to descend in the forest, and to bring that forward, he chooses the long vowel *oo*. I set the poem down first in English, simply for the meaning; and then in German for the meaning and the sound-work.

Over all the hilltops
Silence,
Among all the treetops
You feel hardly
A breath moving.
The birds fall silent in the woods.
Simply wait! Soon
You too will be silent.

In German the *oo* sound shines thorugh.

Über allen Gipfeln
Ist Ruh,
In allen Wipfeln
Spürest du
Kaum einen Hauch:
Die Vögelein schweigen im Walde.
Warte nur! Balde
Ruhest du auch.

Goethe offers the sound *oo* five times in eight short lines, two of them in the last line. By doing so, he affects the listener's body directly, and one falls into the sort of minor trance that allows one to take the "quiet" or "silence" or "stillness" into the heart.

Ancient traditions suggest that each of the seven long vowels tends to produce utterly different or distinct motions of the body. We won't go over those speculations here, but the reader can pronounce *oh* slowly, and see what his or her arms want to do. The sound *oh* apparently makes the body long for enclosure, devotion, holding, and the arms may move to suggest that.

Most ancient texts tend to declare that the seven major vowels symbolize "the primary sounds emitted by the seven heavenly bodies." The long *oh* as in *holy* is the sound of Saturn; *ai*, as we mentioned, is the sun, *ee* is the sound of Venus, and so on.

We recall that Rimbaud, who became aware of these old traditions, assigned in a sonnet written about 1870, colors to the vowels: A *noir*, E *blanc*, I *rouge*, U *vert*, O *bleu*.

Finally, we must mention that many scholars in this field find that the long vowels can be associated fruitfully with one of the prime notes in our typical musical scale. Here we see how the colorful attention to long vowels leads directly and passionately to music, a connection that most contemporary poetry in America and Europe has utterly lost.

There is something delicious about playing with these seven vowels and noticing how one's own body wants to respond to them. Why do you need to study vowels? Because the chiming of sounds in poetry leads us out of the practical reason and into the joy of music. Sometimes in Africa you will hear in a ceremony a speaker pronouncing long vowels so slowly that the body has a chance to give its response.

If you're interested in this matter, you could read Joscelyn Godwin's book, a lively history of these speculations, from the Egyptians to the Celts, called *The Mystery of the Seven Holy Vowels*.

SOUL WEIGHT

For any clump of words to cease being good writing, and to become poetry, we notice the words have to have some psychic weight. Because the creative writing industry has a desire to graduate two or three hundred officially registered veterinarians—I mean poets—each year, a lot of bad poetry gets certified in this country. Hundreds of theses should be rejected by graduate writing programs each year on the grounds that the manuscripts have no discernable psychic weight.

This is a touchy matter, and we probably need someone with more tact than I to define psychic weight. When we call some writing "adolescent," we are usually referring to the lack of psychic weight, even though the work in question may have a lot of pain. When we call a school of poetry "witty," we usually signal that we are going to exempt those poets from the standards just mentioned. We enjoy reading poems that have no discernable psychic weight—that's a lot of fun, like going to the mall.

The weight of the soul is as important in fiction as it is in poetry. We probably all remember Kafka's tale about a son, who, disliked by his father, turned one day into a beetle and began to live under his bed. That single sentence has huge soul weight. We recall that the father returned unexpectedly and found his son—in beetle form—climbing up the wall. The father threw an apple at him, which permanently dented the son's back. This apple, which is apparently brought in from the Garden of Eden story, leads us to the conclusion that a detail drawn from mythology sometimes coincides in great art with psychic weight. Of course the presence of myth does not insure such a thing—mythology can be dished out in an academic, weightless way like anything else. But the soul weight which we feel in Homer and Horace and Rilke is indelibly associated with the mythologies they love. I'll set down a poem by the Spanish poet Antonio Machado; and you'll hear the weight and liveliness of mythology come into the last line.

> The wind one brilliant day, called
> to my soul with an aroma of jasmine.
>
> "In return for this odor of my jasmine,
> I'd like all the odor of your roses."

"I have no roses; I have no flowers.
All the flowers in my garden are dead."

"Then I'll take the waters of the fountains,
and the yellow leaves and the dried-up petals."

The wind left. . . . I wept. I said to my soul,
"What have you done with the garden entrusted to you?"

We notice the garden arrives with a small "g" first; then as we read the poem a second time, we sense a large "G." We have gone from a personal garden to a religious garden. Much recent confessional poetry fails to achieve psychic weight because it stays in the personal garden. Psychic weight does not require catastrophe.

Machado's friend, Juan Ramón Jiménez, simply contrasts the social personality with the "true"—great— personality, and it happens.

I am not I.
I am this one
Walking beside me whom I do not see,
Whom at times I manage to visit
And at other times I forget.
The one who forgives, sweet, when I hate.
The one who remains silent when I talk.
The one who takes a walk when I am indoors.
The one who will remain standing when I die.

Scholars recently discovered a few "Round-Dances" associated with secret Christian worship in the third and fourth centuries in Rome. The discovery includes poems. Here are a few sequences that were apparently spoken by dancers:

I will wound, and I will be wounded.
I will be saved, and I will save.

The small "I" says "I will be saved," and the large "I" says, "I will save."

I will be begotten, and I will beget.
I will hear, and I will be heard.
I will adorn, and I will be adorned.
I will be watched, and I will watch.

The recent movement in the U.S. to adopt pills, and so move away from psychology and mythology is an ominous development, because it is psychology and mythology that have always led us along on the path from the small "I" to the large "I."

If we return to the Antonio Machado poem for a moment, we notice how little judgment there is in it. After Machado confesses that most of the flowers in his garden are dead, the wind doesn't judge him; it simply remarks that it will take the withered leaves and the yellow petals and the waters from the fountain. Machado does not judge himself either for having failed to tend the flowers that were entrusted to him. He simply asks himself: "What have you done with the Garden that was entrusted to you?"

Psychic weight often occurs when religious longings are taken seriously Basho, whose garden lay near a Buddhist temple, said:

The temple bell bell stops.
But the sound keeps coming
out of the flowers.

Thoreau's writing often has terrific soul weight, perhaps because, like Basho, he is defending the religious quality of nature. You may recall that when Thoreau was dying, a visitor to his bed asked him how he stood with Christ. He said, "A snowstorm is more to me than Christ." When the Japanese poet Shiki died in the middle of winter, friends found his death poem under his pillow. It said:

I keep asking
how deep
the snow is now.

We notice little judgment in Van Gogh and almost none in Rembrandt. Even Judas is treated with tenderness by Rembrandt.

On the other hand, some judgment of a culture, if done fairly and with passionate dispassion, so to speak, can achieve soul weight. The last line of Robert Lowell's Boston poem reads:

> A savage servility slides by on grease.

When a poem says things that we know need to be said, it has content; but often soul weight shows itself by things that do not need to be said. Sometimes we wish they hadn't been said, as when Robert Creeley says at the end of a poem:

> Saith perversity, the willful,
> the magnanimous cruelty,
> which is in me
> like a hill.

Psychic weight is one of the gifts given to a work of art by the poet's ability to grieve. We remember that the ancients admired so much in art the quality called *gravitas*. We can hear gravity in the word, and grave, and even the heaviness of pregnancy. These lines of Neruda have gravitas:

> I walk through afternoons, I arrive
> full of mud and death,
> dragging along the earth and its roots,
> and its indistinct stomach in which corpses
> are sleeping with wheat,
> metals, and pushed-over elephants.
>
> But above all there is a terrifying,
> a terrifying deserted dining room. . . .
> and around it there are expanses,
> sunken factories, pieces of timber
> which I alone know,
> because I am sad, and because I travel,
> and I know the earth, and I am sad.

Rilke says:

Rejoicing has lost her doubts, and Longing broods on her error,
Only Grief still learns; she spends the whole night
Counting up our evil inheritance with her small hands.

Cesar Vallejo says:

They'll say that we have a lot
Of grief in one eye, and a lot of grief
In the other also, and when they look
A lot of grief in both . . .
Well then! . . . Wonderful! . . . Then . . .Don't say a word!

Have we said enough about soul weight? It often lifts ordinary writing into poetry. With some practice, one can develop a taste for psychic weight and for grief. The poetry of the United States has never been very welcoming to grief, and our culture in general avoids it. Television provides laugh tracks every 30 seconds. What we call "Language" poetry avoids the language of grief. American poets don't receive much encouragement in intensifying their poetry so that it goes over the line. But Mirabai and Hafez, Leopardi and Neruda, Vallejo and Akhmatova do give such encouragement. Jane Kenyon listened to Akhmatova, and wrote some great poetry. The enemy of psychic weight is fashion, but fashion doesn't last, grief does. The ones born after us will be interested in whether there is any grief in your poems.

OBEYING THE URGE TO FORM THAT IS IN NATURE

A nutty assumption which pervades much American thought about poetry is that form will hobble our free spirits. But once you've watched several thousand hours of television, one might ask, "What free spirit?"

In any event, nature looks at form differently. Form is something playful which actually increases one's chances of remaining alive in a dangerous world. Form is not a thing invented by human beings. On the contrary, nature seems always to be thinking about form. The clamshell makes its shape with a series of elegant repetitions. Each object you find on the beach or in the woods is a masterpiece of achieved form. Only creatures with achieved form live, whether it be a stingray or a hummingbird or some snake with elegantly repeated scales going on for ten feet.

Poets of my own generation were able to see the debate about form in poetry play out during the late 50s and the early 60s. There was so much chaos during the Second World War that I think it's no accident that a few poets beginning to publish as the war ended brought classical form back into their poems. Richard Wilbur would be an example. His first book, *The Beautiful Changes,* was persistent in form and grateful to form.

One wading a Fall meadow finds on all sides
The Queen Anne's Lace lying like lilies
On water; it glides
So from the walker, it turns
Dry grass to a lake, as the slightest shade of you
Valleys my mind in fabulous blue Lucernes.

The beautiful changes as a forest is changed
By a chameleon's tuning his skin to it;
As a mantis, arranged
On a green leaf, grows
Into it, makes the leaf leafier, and proves
Any greenness is deeper than anyone knows.

Your hands hold roses always in a way that says
They are not only yours; the beautiful changes

In such kind ways,
Wishing ever to sunder
Things and things' selves for a second finding, to lose
For a moment all that it touches back to wonder.

Robert Lowell published *Lord Weary's Castle* the previous year, 1946. Its opening poem, "The Exile's Return," describes a German coming back to his occupied village.

There mounts in squalls a sort of rusty mire,
Not ice, not snow, to leaguer the Hôtel
De Ville, where braced pig-iron dragons grip
The blizzard to their rigor mortis. A bell
Grumbles when the reverberations strip
The thatching from its spire,
The search-guns click and spit and split up timber
And nick the slate roofs on the Holstenwall
Where torn-up tilestones crown the victor. Fall
And winter, spring and summer, guns unlimber
And lumber down the narrow gabled street
Past your gray, sorry and ancestral house
Where the dynamited walnut tree
Shadows a squat, old, wind-torn gate and cows
The Yankee commandant. You will not see
Strutting children or meet
The peg-leg and reproachful chancellor
With a forget-me-not in his button-hole
Where the unseasoned liberators roll
Into the Market Square, ground arms before
The Rathaus; but already lily-stands
Burgeon the risen Rhineland, and a rough
Cathedral lifts its eye. Pleasant enough,
Voi ch'entrate, and your life is in your hands.

Lord Weary's Castle exploded with chaotic energy; each poem was like a huge horse kept under some faint control by the iambic line.

A wise person said that form works best when it works in contrast to the content. Let's suppose that the form in a poem goes exactly right, and everything in the content, that is to say the poet's life and the world, goes exactly wrong. Here we see Robert Frost. His content is always out of control, on the edge of madness, but the form goes well. "The Draft Horse" is a good example:

With a lantern that wouldn't burn
In too frail a buggy we drove
Behind too heavy a horse
Through a pitch-dark limitless grove.

And a man came out of the trees
And took our horse by the head
And reaching back to his ribs
Deliberately stabbed him dead.

The ponderous beast went down
With a crack of a broken shaft.
And the night drew through the trees
In one long invidious draft.

The most unquestioning pair
That ever accepted fate
And the least disposed to ascribe
Any more than we had to to hate,

We assumed that the man himself
Or someone he had to obey
Wanted us to get down
And walk the rest of the way.

We could say that Robert Frost's madness was private and he could tame it and partly conceal it with meter. He did that all his life. But for many people who are a little younger, the madness—including the insanity of the Second World War—was social. By 1956, ten years after the end of the war, most of the poets in the "1962" generation—Hall, Simpson Kennedy, Anthony Hecht, Aldrienne Rich—had learned iambic pentameter well. The first anthology of that generation was *New Poets of England and America,* published in 1958. One of the editors, Louis Simpson, whose company was nearly wiped out at the Battle of the Bulge, remarked that the sort of experience that meant the most to him was simply not present in any of the poems he and the other editors received and published. In other words, iambic meter as it was used in 1958 took part in concealing dirt and madness. It acted for some as a screen and a filter, and very little hard reality got through.

It is a strange idea, that iambic meter can work to make a contrasting force to the power of private madness, or it can work so as to dull all disturbance and madness down.

A few years later many of these same poets were forced to make that social madness verbal and audible. What else could we do? Galway Kinnell wrote "The Bear," which is mad; Ginsberg wrote "America," which begins, "America, I've given you all and now I'm nothing... / I won't write my poem until I'm in my right mind . . . / I'm sick of your insane demands." Denise Levertov wrote:

> While the war drags on, always worse,
> the soul dwindles sometimes to an ant
> rapid upon the cracked surface . . .

Adrienne Rich said:

> Poetry never stood a chance
> of standing outside history.
> One line typed twenty years ago
> can be blazed on a wall in spray paint
> to glorify art as detachment.

Within a few years, almost every one of the American poets in *New Poets of England and America,* with the exception of John Hollander and Anthony Hecht, abandoned iambic meter. Why did that happen? It's possible we didn't want to follow nineteenth century England in using the iambic meter to diminish the madness. I remember in the early days of my own magazine *The Fifties* and *The Sixties* when we received poems that seemed excessively iambic, we would send, instead of a rejection slip, a little card that said,

This card entitles you to buy the next book
of Alfred Lord Tennyson as soon as it is published.

We received many insulting responses to that, which we enjoyed deeply.

I think my own generation did make some headway in letting the madness be visible. That was true even in Anthony Hecht's case. He has said that his "cumulative sense of these experiences is grotesque beyond anything I could possibly write." In his poem, "More Light! More Light!", published in 1968, he shows that iambic pentameter can deal well with social madness:

We move now to outside a German wood.
Three men are there commanded to dig a hole
In which the two Jews are ordered to lie down
And be buried alive by the third, who is a Pole.

Not light from the shrine at Weimar beyond the hill
Nor light from heaven appeared. But he did refuse.
A Luger settled back deeply in its glove.
He was ordered to change places with the Jews.

Much casual death had drained away their souls.
The thick dirt mounted toward the quivering chin.
When only the head was exposed the order came
To dig him out again and to get back in.

No light, no light in the blue Polish eye.
When he finished a riding boot packed down the earth.
The Luger hovered lightly in its glove.
He was shot in the belly and in three hours bled to death.

No prayers or incense rose up in those hours
Which grew to be years, and every day came mute
Ghosts from the ovens, sifting through crisp air,
And settled upon his eyes in a black soot.

We could say the meter is whole and the content broken. In Robert Duncan's poem on the war, he adopts open form:

> Now Johnson would go up to join the great simulacra of men,
> Hitler and Stalin, to work his fame
> with planes roaring from Guam over Asia,
> all America become a sea of toiling men
> stirrd at his will, which would be a bloated thing,
> drawing from the underbelly of the nation
> such blood and dreams as swell the idiot psyche
> out of its courses into an elemental thing
> until his name stinks with burning meat and heapt honors. . . .
>
> this specter that in the beginning Adams and Jefferson feard and knew
> would corrupt the very body of the nation
> and all our sense of our common humanity,
> this black bile of old evils arisen anew,
> takes over the vanity of Johnson;
> and the very glint of Satan's eyes from the pit of the hell of America's unacknowledged, unrepented crimes that I saw in Goldwater's eyes
> and now shines from the eyes of the President
> in the swollen head of the nation.

In Duncan, though the form is open, the madness of the Vietnam War shines through.

For those unclear about that decade, these details may help as a brief history. Our generation, or most of the poets in it, went to free verse in order to come closer to some madness that the iambic meter could not handle.

It's difficult in any century to find the right form. As I mentioned above, form is something playful which increases your chances of remaining alive in a dangerous world. How does one invent a form? Suppose one is not interested in iambic form but wants some form anyway? What can one do? I'll throw out an idea: If you are not counting anything in your poems, there is no form, no matter how much people talk about "open form." Marianne Moore counted syllables; she didn't care a bit about accents and the number of strong and weak accents; she counted syllables. That brought her poems closer to nature, which, I've said earlier in this essay, always counts.

Perhaps we could stop thinking of certain syllables as being stressed or unstressed; instead one could count them as so many whole notes and so many quarter notes and so many eighth notes. Sidney Lanier wrote about that form of counting, and I recommend his wonderful book, *The Science of English Meter.*

Shakespeare writes:

> That time of year thou mayst in me behold
> When yellow leaves or none, or few, do hang
> Upon those boughs that shake beneath the cold
> Bare ruined choirs, where late the sweet birds sang.

It becomes clear that Shakespeare provides a long vowel in the fourth place and the tenth place in every line. He is definitely counting. The open vowels that we perceive are *year* and *hold, leaves* and *hang, boughs* and *cold, choirs* and *sang.* If we find a tune that fits this poem, we find it fits most of the sonnets that Shakespeare wrote. We might add that a tune helps us to count.

The Greek Alcaic meter, made popular in Greek by Alcaeus, and later brought into the Latin language by Horace, depends on the counting of three different lengths of vowels. Once more, these musical inventions become plausible when the sounds are spoken, or sung. Perhaps a form in English is impossible for those who do not memorize poems and recite or sing them. Tomas Tranströmer has successfully used Alcaic meter in Swedish; you'll find it in *För Levande och Döda,* "Alcaisk."

In the next years, I think we will receive much influence from the poetic forms in the Muslim culture. In classical Persian and Arabic and Urdu poetry, the relative lengths of all the vowels are counted. A Rumi or Hafez poem can be sung immediately. In hundreds of non-English languages, the poets count the long vowels, count the short vowels, count the number of syllables, count even interior rhymes. The small sound units such as *in* and *or* and *an* offer themselves for repetition and counting.

Perhaps I've said enough here to give the flavor of this discipline. The dead won't ask you which prizes you've received; they'll ask you if there is any form in your poems.

LEARNING TO LOVE EXCESS

We have the feeling that ancient poetry was always excessive. *Beowulf* could hardly be described as a moderate poem, following the middle way. Almost every human and non-human creature in it goes over the line on a daily basis. Gilgamesh was out of line—he lacked social boundaries, we are told—and to cure him they brought in Enkidu who was even more excessive! In the *Iliad,* we find men who can kill fifty people out of simple hurt feelings. The dead have a great taste for excess.

In Eric Havelock's marvelous book *Preface to Plato,* he made a few remarks about the nature of a poetry reading in ancient Greece. He said that the Homeric poetry reading worked to bring such a huge presence of grief into the room that it took away grief.

He also observed that in a poetry reading the poet has to provide the initial charge of emotion and energy, and give that out of himself or herself even before the audience has given him or her anything back. That's how a poetry reading works. That's how story-telling works. The powerful Homeric meter, with its carefully registered beats and carefully provided pauses, worked so as to tie the grief into the heartbeat of the listeners. It's as if the mind couldn't reject the excess, because the excess was already in the body.

Perhaps someone should write a history of excess. Those who know Indian ecstatic poetry know that Mirabai is a great warrior against moderation. Jane Hirshfield has translated a poem of hers this way:

> When you offer the Great One your love,
> At the first step your body is crushed.
> Next be ready to offer your head as his seat
> To live in the deer as she runs toward the hunter's call,
> In the partridge that swallows hot coals for the love of the moon. . . .
> Like a bee trapped for life in the closing of the sweet flower,
> Mira has offered herself to her Lord.
> She says: The single lotus will swallow you whole.

Talking to the sort of people (her family) who urge her to reaccept a more ordinary householder's life, she says:

I have felt the swaying of the elephant's shoulders, and now you
want me to climb on a jackass?

Try to be serious.

(translated by RB)

Kabir, slightly older than Mirabai, speaks in the same immediate way:

The idea that the soul will join with the ecstatic
just because the body is rotten—
that is all fantasy.
What is found now is found then.
If you find nothing now,
you will simply end up with an apartment in the City of Death.
If you make love with the divine now, in the next life you will have
the face of satisfied desire.

(translated by RB)

This habit of excessiveness carries right through into the 19th century. Ghalib ends one of his poems:

The lightning that fell on Moses should have fallen on Ghalib.
You know we always adjust the quantity of the liquor to the quality
of the drinker.

(translated by RB and Sunil Dutta)

Because we are familiar now with Rumi's sweet overstatements, we might imagine that this art is particular to him; it has actually been a common form of speech among literate Shiites through the whole Muslim world for centuries. When we compare our sensible American poems, we are the ones who seem backward.

Hafez says:

Don't expect obedience, promise-keeping, or rectitude
From me; I'm drunk. I have been famous for carrying
A wine pitcher around since the First Covenant with Adam.

When we look at Shakespeare, we might ask: "Why do all the characters in Shakespeare's plays speak so wildly?" It is because he knew of this tradition. The Italians in *Orlando Furioso,* in Petrarch, in love sonnets, carried that speech of divine excess into France and England. The complicated syntax of the Renaissance actually supported that wildness. Even the minor characters in Shakespeare speak fabulously, outrageously, grandiloquently, rolling along in the delight of the immoderate.

The *Furioso* tradition began to dim in the 18th century; and during that century the popularity of Shakespeare fell sharply.

Samuel Johnson, an otherwise wonderfully intelligent man, is not very susceptible to excess. He's talking here of bad writing in general, but there's a sting in "invention":

> Why this wild strain of imagination found reception so long, in polite and learned ages, is not easy to conceive; but we cannot wonder, that, while readers could be procured, the authors were willing to continue it: For when a man had, by practice, gained some fluency of language, he had no farther care than to retire to his closet, to let loose his invention, and heat his mind with incredibilities; and a book was produced without fear of criticism, without the toil of study, without knowledge or nature, or acquaintance with life.

Pope is often belabored about the shoulders for writing this line:

> The proper study of mankind is man.

He probably deserved it. He went on:

> The bliss of man (could pride that blessing find)
> Is not to act or think beyond mankind;
> No powers of body or of soul to share,
> But what his nature and his state can bear.
> Why has not man a microscopic eye?
> For this plain reason, man is not a fly.

Well, that settles it. Jonathan Swift, like all the Irish, has secret stores of the unnamable, and he pays no attention to moderation. By the early years of the 19th century, English poetry still had not recovered the skill of excess. Blake stood out by his love for it, and that love is one reason so few Londoners would buy his paintings, or give honor to his poems. But he was unequivocal and unrepentent; he was in line with ancient literature.

> My mother groaned, my father wept,
> Into the dangerous world I leapt,
> Helpless, naked, piping loud
> Like a fiend hid in a cloud.

We know his aphorisms:

> The tigers of wrath are wiser than the horses of instruction.
> He whose face gives no light shall never become a star.
> The road of excess leads to the palace of wisdom.
> Drive your cart and your plow over the bones of the dead.
> The roaring of lions, the howling of wolves, the raging of the stormy sea, and the destructive sword, are portions of eternity, too great for the eye of man.
> You never know what is enough unless you know what is more than enough.

We can say that in the English language, Blake is, after Shakespeare, the greatest carrier of excess, and its greatest defender. Beautiful excess belongs to solitude and the company of geniuses.

> The Prophets Isaiah and Ezekiel dined with me, and I asked them how they dared so roundly to assert that God spoke to them; and whether they did not think at the time that they would be misunderstood, & so be the cause of imposition. . . .
>
> I then asked Ezekiel why he eat dung, & lay so long on his right & left side? he answer'd, "the desire of raising other men into a perception of the infinite: this the North American tribes practice, & is he honest who resists his genius or conscience only for the sake of present ease or gratification?"

In the U.S., both Emily Dickinson and Whitman stood up for the intemperate and the exhorbitant, for the inordinate and the overwrought. But during the 20th century it was in the Spanish language—both in Spain and in South America—that the longing to go beyond measure, to give more than enough, to "kill the slain," which was the character of much ancient literature, returned.

If you're looking for excess, Cesar Vallejo has it:

Well, on the day I was born,
God was sick.

(Translated by James Wright)

He also began a poem:

I will die in Paris, on a rainy day,
on some day I can already remember.

(translated by RB and John Knoepfle)

The purpose of powerful assertion at the beginning of a poem is so that one's deeper emotions will be called out. In our culture, flooded with mediocre art, it's perfectly possible to write poetry your whole life without ever being asked to bring forward the intense emotions that are somewhere inside of you—those emotions that love to be seen, those emotions we are each afraid of, those emotions that will curse us and poison us if we don't honor them by speaking them, those emotions that will bless us if we do speak them.

Some of us have a desire for life to end and the whole world to end and everything to die. We can watch Cesar Vallejo edge toward it:

And what if after so many words,
the word itself doesn't survive!
And what if after so many wings of birds,
the stopped bird doesn't survive!
It would be better then, really,
if it were all swallowed up, and let's end it!

(Translated by RB and Douglas Lawder)

He sometimes opens a poem with an assertion so outrageous that it can only be answered by intense emotion.

> I have a terrible fear of being an animal of white snow.

If one begins a poem with that intensity, one can't go on later and be reasonable and complain about your parents. We want poets to tell the truth. But he is not trying to tell the truth. That is for writers. To make poetry means that you need to go over the line, to be not sensible but arresting, not to be acceptable but to be unforgettable.

My very insistence that excess is one of the qualities that distinguishes poetry from good writing is excessive itself. But still, I want to say that most of the greatest poetry in the twentieth century has kept the intemperate at its center. Here's Pablo Neruda, writing in 1933, a poem to which he gave an English title, "Walking Around":

> It so happens I am sick of being a man.
> And it happens that I walk into tailorshops and movie houses
> dried up, waterproof, like a swan made of felt
> steering my way in a water of wombs and ashes. . . .
>
> It so happens I am sick of my feet and my nails
> and my hair and my shadow.
> It so happens I am sick of being a man.
>
> Still it would be marvelous
> to terrify a law clerk with a cut lily,
> or kill a nun with a blow on the ear.

It's the job of the poet to give the initial charge of emotion and energy at the start of the poem. Lorca says:

> To take the wrong road
> is to arrive at the snow
> and to arrive at the snow
> is to get down on all fours for twenty centuries and eat the grasses
> of the cemeteries. . . .

He goes on:

> Dead people hate the number two,
> but the number two makes women drop off to sleep,
> and since women are afraid of light,
> light shudders when it has to face the roosters,
> and since all roosters know is how to fly over the snow
> we will have to get down on all fours and eat the grasses
> of the cemeteries forever.

He begins another poem:

> Get up,
> My friend, so you can hear the Assyrian hound howling.

Later in the poem he says:

> I loved a child for a long time
> who had a tiny feather on his tongue
> and we lived a hundred years inside a knife.

He wouldn't have arrived at that marvelous line about the feather on the tongue if the poem hadn't started with that high energy. The energy has to come in on the very first line.

The aim of poetry is to achieve an excess that is more interesting and more nourishing than truth. Eliot in "East Coker" says:

> The whole earth is our hospital
> Endowed by the ruined millionaire.

He is a worthy continuer of the old traditions we see first in Gilgamesh, Homer, and Beowulf. Among later poets, Ginsberg has made some true sallies into excess, as well as Thomas McGrath, and in a different mode Galway Kinnell. Lifting your writing up into poetry with the help of this discipline is not something which is easy to do. But English has so much energy in it now, that I think this lifting up is perfectly possible.

TALKING IN SUCH A WAY THAT THE HEART CAN HEAR

This particular skill seems to be open to beginners often, more often than professional writers. Children in the second or third grade are often geniuses in this sort of thing. As writers of my generation grew up, it was not a skill that was much admired among critics. What was admired was paradox, tension, multiple meanings, "the seven types of ambiguity," and the secret contrast between surface content and hidden content. Teachers could easily find these qualities in John Donne, in Yeats, in John Crowe Ransom, in Stevens and Pound. I still love those paradoxical complications, and the teachers' emphasis on them made us close readers of any text, and helped us to stay away a bit from the simple-mindedness that always seems to be a part of North American culture. But as poets we had to learn on our own about a quiet voice speaking to someone listening. Luckily, Chinese poetry has always modeled this skill well. The anthology of poetry by Robert Payne called *The White Pony* became a Bible for many of us. I'll recite to you one poem from that book.

Everyone knew there was a certain mountain, all solid stone, out of which a river flowed. In spring, one could see peach blossoms floating on that river. Li Po said:

> If you ask me why I dwell among green mountains,
> I would laugh silently; my soul is serene.
> The peach blossom follows the moving water.
> There is another heaven and earth beyond the world of men.

Emily Dickinson said,

> Poetry is all we know of heaven
> And all we need of hell.

We cannot imagine either of these poems being shouted. When we begin speaking of this skill, the voice naturally drops and we feel an achieved intimacy. Chinese poets have a genius for this tone. Perhaps the tone developed out of the circumstance that all classical Chinese poems were sung to a tune, so the mood was something like:

> Greensleeves are all my joy,
> And Greensleeves are my delight.

Songs are almost always directed at the heart. You can hear it in Leadbelly's song "Goodnight Irene":

> Last Saturday night I got married
> Me and my wife settled down
> Now me and my wife are parted
> I'm going to take little stroll downtown
>
> Sometimes I live in the country,
> Sometimes I live in town,
> Sometimes I get a great notion
> To jump in the river and drown.

We also notice a beautiful playfulness often in poems aimed at the heart. Playful words are willing to live happily with some tune. Such songs are easygoing. Bob Dylan and Leadbelly and Li Po are all alike in that way.

In the west, Kenneth Rexroth was one of the poets who led the way out of the "seven types of ambiguity." Here is "Fifty":

> Rainy skies, misty mountains,
> The old year ended in storms.
> The new year starts the same way.
> All day, from far out at sea,
> Long winged birds soared in the
> Rushing sky. Midnight breaks with
> Driving clouds and plunging moon,
> Rare vasts of endless stars.
> My fiftieth year has come.

Gary Snyder learned it from him. Gary heard this old farm worker who was working with him say one day,

"I first bucked hay when I was seventeen.
I thought, that day I started,
I sure would hate to do this all my life.
And dammit, that's just what
I've gone and done."

When *News of the Universe* came out, I dedicated the book to Rexroth, adapting a portion of a poem Machado wrote to his teacher: "One day the master imagined a new blossoming." Later I heard that a young poet brought the new book to Rexroth and gave it to him; when Rexroth read the dedication, tears came down his face. We understand that the community of poets is a genuine community.

Our subject is talking so that the other can hear. Ruth Stone, who is a little like Grace Paley, describes sitting with her daughter in a parking lot, having some doughnuts and coffee:

We are silent.
For a moment the wall between us
opens to the universe;
then closes.
And you go on saying
you do not want to repeat my life.

A great master of this skill is Etheridge Knight. He said:

This poem
This poem
This poem / is / for me
        and my woman
        and the yesterdays
when she opened
        to me like a flower
        But I fell on her
        like a stone
I fell on her like a stone . . .

4
And now—in my 40th year
            I have come here
to this House of Feelings
to this Singing Sea
and I and I / must admit
that the sea in me
            has fallen / in love
with the sea in you
because the sea
that now sings / in you
            is the same sea
that nearly swallowed you—
            and me too.

We know that American poets currently have great skill in this quality which we call talking to the heart. Let's name a few others besides Etheridge Knight: Galway Kinnell, Mary Oliver, William Stafford, James Wright, Sharon Olds, and many more. A typical poem by Russell Edson will open:

"John, come on down here and hurt your father."

This ability to touch the heart is a gift of North and South America these days. One could say that French surrealism did considerable harm to the French poets' ability to talk to the heart. At this moment, poetry is in a low state in France, both in its writers and its readers; and the tendency of the French to become rhetorical and full of intellectual affects must have some responsibility here.

Some confessional poets in this country have missed the heart by going into the longing to judge. Both Sylvia Plath and Anne Sexton are constantly pointing out flawed people, parents, or country club types. By contrast, the contemporary Guatemalan poet Humberto Ak'abal, whose first book in English has now been printed, has, being Mayan, a thousand reasons to call down judgment on others, but he does not do so. He stays in the place where he can talk quietly. Here are three brief poems of his translated by Miguel Rivera:

Poets are born old;
with the passing of the years
we make ourselves into children.

☆

Shadow:
little night
at the foot of any tree.

☆

In the high hours of the night
stars get naked
and bathe in the rivers.

Owls desire them,
the little feathers on their heads
stand up.

This is the closest he gets to judgment:

In the churches
you can only hear the prayer
of the trees
converted into pews.

One reason Rumi has become so popular in the U.S. is that Coleman Barks has put him into the "spoken American" that American poets have developed over the last fifty years; and the translated poems speak beautifully to the heart.

A night full of talking that hurts,
my worst held-back secrets. Everything
has to do with loving and not loving.
This night will pass.
Then we have work to do.

*

A chickpea leaps almost over the rim of the pot
where it's being boiled.

"Why are you doing this to me?"

The cook knocks it down with a ladle.

"Don't you try to jump out.
You think I'm torturing you,
I'm giving you flavor,
so you can mix with spices and rice
and be the lovely vitality of a human being.

Remember when you drank rain in the garden.
That was for this."

Grace first Sexual pleasure,
then a boiling new life begins,
and the Friend has something good to eat.

In Canada, Alden Nowlan, whose poems are still too little known here, is a great master. In his poem, "He Sits Down on the Floor of a School for the Retarded," he talks of a young retarded woman who has sat down next to him. She says, "Hold me."

"Hold me," she says again. What does it matter
what anybody thinks? . . .

It's what we all want, in the end,
to be held, merely to be held,
to be kissed (not necessarily with the lips,
for every touching is a kind of kiss).
Yes, it's what we all want, in the end,
not to be worshipped, not to be admired,
not to be famous, not to be feared,

not even to be loved, but simply to be held.

I'd say that among the six skills I'm mentioning in this essay, this skill, talking to the heart in a way that it can hear, is in some ways the most important of them all. It carries much of the genius of contemporary American poetry.

This is the end of our little excursion into skills that poets of the past knew, skills which are not always taught in the writing workshops, or are not all visible today. Another poet might have chosen six utterly different disciplines, and that would be all right with me. Perhaps if I wrote this essay next week, I might choose six different ones myself.

WHAT THE IMAGE CAN DO

I.

Poets my age and younger have probably placed too much emphasis on the image in recent years, too much, that is, in relation to the other powers of poetry, such as the dance of pitch, discourse, narrative, sound, and weight of thought. My own overemphasis on image has been partly at fault for that, but one could also say that other critics who should have balanced or corrected the overemphasis on image did not appear. I am glad of the new criticism by Robert Hass, Charles Molesworth, Frederick Turner, all practicing poets. The image brings so much moistness to a poem that it cannot, I think, be overpraised, but when a poet works on it solely or mainly he or she may, without intending it, let other beings in the poem starve. It's possible that Williams starved the resonating sound and thought areas of his poetry by working so doggedly on colloquial or spoken language.

The image belongs with the simile, the metaphor, and the analogy. Shelley said, "Metaphorical language marks the before unapprehended relations of things." Owen Barfield remarks in his marvelous book called *Poetic Diction* (which is about many other things as well) that he would like to alter only one detail of Shelley's sentence. He would change "before unapprehended relationships" to "forgotten relationships." He says that ancient man stood in the center of a wheel of rays coming to him from objects. As an example of a "forgotten relationship" we could mention the relationship between the woman's body and a tree. Medieval alchemists created drawings showing a woman taking a baby from a tree trunk. We all know other examples. Many relationships then have been forgotten — by us. They can be recovered. "For though they were never yet apprehended they were at one time seen," Barfield says. "And imagination can see them again." When a poet creates a true image, he is gaining knowledge; he is bringing up into consciousness a connection that has been forgotten, perhaps for centuries.

I think Barfield's understanding of the image is tremendous. The power of the image is the power of seeing resemblances. That discipline is essential to the growth of intelligence, to everyone's intelligence, but especially to the poet's intelligence. Emerson, who was Thoreau's master, said, talking of true analogies:

> It is easily seen that there is nothing lucky or capricious in these analogies, but that they are constant, and pervade nature. These are not the dreams of a few poets, here and there, but man is an analogist, and studies relations in all objects. He is placed in the center of beings, and a ray of relation passes from every other being to him.

The question then we have to ask of an image when we write it is, Does this image retrieve a forgotten relationship or is it merely a silly juxtaposition, which is amusing but nothing more?

II.

Barfield maintains that every true image — every image that moves us — or moves the memory — contains a concealed analogical sequence. "Analogy" holds the word "logic" in it. He believes that the imagination calls on logic to help it create the true image and so to recover the forgotten relationship. He gives these lines of Shelley as text:

> My soul is an enchanted boat,
> Which, like a sleeping swan, doth float
> Upon the silver waves of thy sweet singing.

I'll try to work out the analogy implied. This is a possibility:

> My soul is to your singing
> as a boat is to water.

That's all right, but maybe a little bare.

> My soul is to your sounds
> as a sleeping swan is to water.

That sequence is better, because it includes the idea of enchantment, which has a secret resonance with "sleeping swan."

A great image contains logic, that is, thinking. One has to be intelligent to create an image and intelligent to understand it.

Two other lines Barfield quotes, from Shakespeare, are more mysterious:

> What is your substance, whereof are you made,
> That millions of strange shadows on you tend?

We can feel enormous energy enter the poem with the word "millions." The energy is thought-energy that Shakespeare gave to the creation of the image. Barfield remarks that "sometimes in retracing the path back to the hidden analogy, a great deal of abstraction is necessary before we can arrive at the ratio." The ratio is his word for the sequence of analogies that we unravel slowly, but that the imagination saw in a flash as it was writing the poem. What is the hidden ratio that underlies Shakespeare's image? We can try this:

> Your inner personality is to ordinary personality
> as a great magnet is to an ordinary stone.

That's possible, but it doesn't feel quite right. Let's try this:

> Your substance is to the mysterious inner being
> as a great medium is to ghosts longing to speak.

That's better. Barfield however suggests this:

> My experience of you is to the rest of my experience
> as the sun is to the earth.

Delving like this makes clear that the true image has thought in it; complicated analogical, even logical, perceptions fuse with imagination to make a strong image.

It is particularly important at this moment to recognize the complicated power of the image in order to counter the disparagement of image that we find in critics who favor discourse. Many critics who defend discursive poetry — which I like as well — attack the image by maintaining that it often ignores intelligence. One young poet declared recently that the image denies "what can only be called intelligence, and the possibility of reflection upon experience, the ability to make sense of our histories, our limits as well as our possibilities." Such a poet or critic may follow this attack with an image poem triumphantly made up in three minutes, as if composing images were easy, as if any high-school student could write images as well as Shakespeare or Trakl.

I like intelligence when it appears debating both sides of a question in the discursive poem, and I also like intelligence as it appears in an image. I would say that my respect for the image's power has deepened, rather than diminished, in the last few years.

III.

Having called attention to Owen Barfield's praise of the logical thought underpinning a genuine image, I'll end this piece by making a distinction of my own between two sorts of images.

We know that the image merges worlds: Shakespeare with his "millions of strange shadows" joins the invisible world to the visible world. The true image has a room where each may live. An image may link the world of the dead with the world of the living. Trakl wrote:

The oaks turn green
in such a ghostly way over the forgotten footsteps of the dead.

It may connect what we know with what we don't. Emily Dickinson wrote:

Exultation is the going
Of the inland soul to sea,
Past the houses—past the headlands—
Into deep Eternity.

It may join science and history. Blake said,

The Atoms of Democritus
And Newton's Particles of light
Are sands upon the Red Sea shore
Where Israel's tents do shine so bright.

Bert Meyers, the Los Angeles poet, writes about his days as a frame maker:

At dusk I drive home

the proud cattle of my hands.

The body let the cattle be its fatigue, and the spirit contributed its exultation.

These are all examples of the image as container. We don't need to be reminded that the alchemists had to create strong containers in order to fuse substances. We could say that the image fuses two sorts of consciousness in its strong container.

A second sort of image resembles a pole or an arrow more than a container. An image of this sort reaches out from human language to touch something else not entirely human. For example, if we imagine each sentence and each phrase in Blake's "Tiger" to point to a single power outside the poem, then the images that make up the poem are not so much containers as a verbal arm reaching out to touch the nonhuman:

What the hammer? what the chain?
In what furnace was thy brain?
What the anvil? what dread grasp
Dare its deadly terrors clasp?

The poem refers well beyond the animal.

The power of a myth depends on it embodying at least one of those "arm" images. An arm image, once found, can persist for centuries, passing from religion to religion, and worshippers never exhaust its possibilities. Yeats in one of his late poems has Mary say,

The terror of all terrors that I bore
The Heavens in my womb.

Yeats's image is an arm or a pole or a bridge. There is terror in the image because someone is approaching us over the bridge. We don't experience the bridge image as logical or analogical but as terrifying, numinous.

We remember that Hades in the myth of Persephone burst up from below, and Persephone either willingly, as the old texts have it, or unwillingly, as the later texts have it, went down with him. When searchers found the opening into the earth, her footprints were gone, obliterated by the footprints of pigs, for it turned out that a herd of pigs had gone down with the two. There is a terror in that image; and it reminds us of the pigs that Christ drove over a cliff.

Images of the bridge or arm sort carry us to conscious or superconscious matter. We feel that touching of superconscious matter in events that happen "synchronistically": after longing all week for a certain book, we walk into a stranger's house and see it lying open on the table. Physicists who conducted the "Copenhagen experiments" found out that they could plot either the speed of a subatomic particle or its position. If the experimenter aimed to know its position, it would appear, but somehow it hadn't traveled there.

The bridge or arm images work against the notion that human intelligence is alone in the universe, isolated, and unchangeably remote from the natural world. Yeat's image reaches out with the left hand and touches a pregnant woman's conscious stomach and reaches out with the right and touches the superconscious "Heavens."

The Norwegians created an arm or pole image for Thor: lightning over a ripe barley field. Here the left hand touches the tips of the barley, and the right hand the superconscious energy they called Thor. The ancient Gothic imagination was unwilling to accept the severe categorization of inner and outer, divine and animal, intelligent and brute, that Aristotle and later Descartes acquiesce in. This Gothic union, or oneness of worlds, is what Wallace Stevens suggests by the word "Harmonium." He stated his belief that sooner or later human beings will reappear who can grasp this doubly conscious world:

> And in their chant shall enter, voice by voice,
> The windy lake wherein their lord delights,
> The trees, like seraphim and echoing hills
> That choir among themselves long afterward.

These images are wild, not domestic. Barfield says that the power that makes us able to touch "the Heavens" and the human skin at the same time is called imagination. This large word has a smaller word "image" in it.

1981, 1989

III.

THE LABOR OF ITS PLAYFULNESS

EDUCATING THE RIDER AND THE HORSE

I.

I have been thinking lately that the poets of my generation have not been very faithful servants of art. What did Yeats say?

> I know what wages beauty gives,
> How hard a life her servant lives,
> Yet praise the winters gone;
> There is not a fool can call me friend.
> And I may dine at journey's end
> With Landor and with Donne.

We have been faithful and intense servants, but what we have served is the intensity of private material. Goethe said something like this: "In a work of art the private material is easiest to understand, the meaning more difficult, and the form still more difficult, and few can fathom it."

I imagine private material to be close to the chest, perhaps inside the chest; it needs the bone protection; and I imagine meaning to be floating several feet out from the chest, between the chest and the human community. Meaning is a wild thing, passed to us through centuries by old men and old women, it is knowledge passed hand to hand, so to speak, and something secret comes with it. If we follow the metaphor, form then would live still farther out, still farther from the chest, and would be still wilder. That may be why it is more difficult to understand. This view comes as a surprise to me because I have often thought of form as a prison, a kind of dungeon in which heart material gets imprisoned. If I have been wrong on that, then I need to find a way to speak of form so that its wild or intense quality becomes clear.

II.

In imagining form as wild, we don't get much help from the writers of standard texts on form. I. A. Richards comments in his *Principles of Literary Criticism*:

> The whole conception of meter as "uniformity in variety," a kind of mental drill in which words, those erratic and varied things, do their best to behave as though they were all the same, with certain concessions, licenses and equivalences allowed, should nowadays be obsolete . . . though it has been knocked on the head vigorously enough by Professor Saintsbury and others, it is as difficult to kill as Punch.

Paul Fussell, writing thirty years later, says,

> Meter inheres in more or less regular linguistic rhythm; or we can say that talk about meter is a way of describing our awareness of those rhythmical patterns in poetic language which can be measured and formulated. Perhaps when we speak of meter we mean the "ideal" patterns which poetic rhythms approximate. That is, if meter is regarded as an ideal and thus invariable formal pattern, then rhythm moves toward meter the closer it approaches regularity and predictability. (*Poetic Meter and Poetic Form*)

C. S. Lewis in "Meter" says, "When we ask for the meter of a poem we are asking for a paradigm." W. K. Wimsatt, Jr., and Monroe Beardsley, in "The Concept of Meter: An Exercise in Abstraction," declare that "meter is something which for the most part inheres in language precisely at that level of linguistic organization which grammars and dictionaries and elementary rhetoric can successfully cope with."

Most critics then, as I. A. Richards complains, use the mechanical model when they talk of form, and omit what we could call the organic model. The mechanical model is taken from human economy, and the other from the economy of nature. We could easily oversimplify the distinction, but we'll stick with it a few minutes. The mechanical model — a predictable paradigm, for example — depends on certain mechanical repetitions human beings have achieved, in clocks and other geared machines, in belted factories and so on. The second or organic form draws from the success nature has had in its plant and animal adaptation. It is the second form that would deserve the term "wild" because the word "wild" refers to what humans have not domesticated, what is still receiving nourishment from nature.

III.

A living animal's body reconciles various energies. We note that "form" is close to "shape," and both words suggest a body that holds in balance certain energies, even conflicting energies, as a snail shell reconciles both circular and linear drives. A good body does not destroy the energies or allow them to destroy the body. Wallace Stevens said, "I placed a jar in Tennessee." A shape is a container but it also implies order, for example, a beginning, middle, and end, something that chaos does not have. A snail shell certainly has a beginning, middle, and end. We notice that form implies some sort of return. We say the universe has form because the Dog Star returns, the moon returns to full each month, spring returns each year, the salmon return to their rivers. In the snail shell, a certain curve, which can easily be plotted, returns everywhere in the shell.

As primitive animals move toward the mammal form, their adaptation becomes more complicated, and attention is paid to breathing, speed of the heart, heat of the blood. Speed of heartbeat seems associated with the successful adaptation that hummingbirds have made. In the tiger, its interior bone structure, the heartbeat, the lungs, the sinews in legs and neck help it to be a shape that contains fierce energies, and helps it to survive among other fierce energies. By contrast, if we imagine a poem composed in mechanical form, correctly paradigmatic — a villanelle for example — as an animal, it would appear rigid, stiff-kneed, with medieval coloring, and so poorly adapted to the ground and trees around it that it would not survive the winter.

If we imagine one of Whitman's long poems as an animal, it would be an animal about a mile and half long with not enough bone structure between head and tail, big in the stomach, and so cumbersome it would be killed by the first lion that noticed it on the grassy plain.

The animal that survives in the wild, the tiger, the horse, the wolverine, has just the right number of bones, just the right number of feet, a good balance of lung and heart, and just the right number of vertebrae. Moreover, it somehow fits the continent on which it lives.

So when we speak of form as a wildness and consider a poem's form as drawn from the careful economy of nature, we imagine the wild poem as an animal that moves fast, can leap in the air, escape from professors or metricists, and live for generations, even during the leanest climatic times.

I maintain then that the more form a poem has — I mean living form — the closer it comes to the wild animal.

Supposing that were true, what helps nudge the poem toward gazelle form or wolf form? First, passionate speech. Yeats said, "I love all the arts that can still remind me of their origin among the common people, and my ears are only comfortable when the singer sings as if mere speech had taken fire . . ." If we mumble, and apologize for speaking, we are victims; the lion is not a victim. Rumi says, "You're always most handsome when you're looking for food."

Second, "sentence sound." It is a certain sequence of pitches. Frost describes it this way:

> You recognize the sentence sound in this: You, you . . . ! It is so strong that if you hear it as I do you may have to pronounce the two yous differently. Just so many sentence sounds belong to man as just so many vocal runs belong to one kind of bird. We come into the world with them and create none of them. What we feel as creation is only selection and grouping. We summon them from Heaven knows where under excitement with the audile imagination. And unless we are in an imaginative mood it is no use trying to make them, they will not rise. We can only write the dreary kind of grammatical prose known as professional.

This, Frost said, is "the most important thing I know."

Third, the conscious intensity — not sequence — of pitches. Syllables that rose high, very high, in the old Norse lines the poets called "lifters." We can hear them in *Beowulf*. Sometimes the lifters resemble the peak of a roof, sometimes the dragon prow of a Viking ship that rises and falls. Sounds pronounced naturally in the roof of the mouth, such as "ee," drive the sound up; conviction drives it up; the beat as it arrives helps drive it up. This is mysterious, unquantifiable.

Fourth, the animal rhythm that arrives over and above the human rhythm laid down. Milton in some passages of "Paradise Lost" provides a domestic rhythm of five beats, a kind of walking. His ear can hear over that a rhythm riding on three of these beats, which resembles a man running. Over that his ear can hear a third rhythm laid down on only two of those beats; and that third rhythm gives the feeling of an animal running. The three rhythms running together are too complicated to be paradigms, and our language is not subtle enough to describe them.

Finally, recurrence of vowel and consonant. Anglo-Saxon poetry creates much of its wildness in this way. A study of the way the Norse and Anglo-Saxon poets achieved this is too elaborate to be summed up. But one can say that when a sound is repeated in a certain way, the sound becomes alive and runs away.

IV.

Talking this way we reach the threshold between domestic and wild form. On the threshold we are neither in the house nor out, neither in the conscious world nor the unconscious, neither in this world nor the other world. That is where living form takes the poem. And thresholds belong to all betwixt and between places, to the heron that is neither land bird nor sea bird, to mercury that is neither metal nor liquid.

Ancient Celtic women would sometimes lay hard conditions on a man courting them. Conflicting loyalties and obligations often made serious courting dangerous for both parties. Moreover no woman wants to offer "the friendship of her upper thighs" to a man who can't solve riddles, or is too straitlaced, or has no playfulness in his soul. So she might say, you can come to me, but neither in the day nor the night, and neither riding nor walking, and you should be neither in the house nor out.

The wise lover might appear at her door then lying across a short pony, with his legs dragging, so he is neither riding nor walking, at dusk, which is neither day nor night; and once he arrived at her door he wouldn't call to her until the pony's front legs were inside the house and the back legs outside. Once he had fulfilled all conditions, they could do what they wished, because they were neither in this world nor the next.

V.

Loving meaning in the way Goethe speaks of means investigating the mythological implications of images in the way Goethe and Yeats actually did. Investigating images and their meaning is education of the rider. Studying how drummers catch fire is educating the horse. Drummers as we know do not aim for the rigid or mechanical paradigm that Fussell and Wimsatt praise as form. There is a place on the threshold then that educates both rider and horse.

When we are on the threshold, we can begin to imagine or reimagine for poetry a form neither reimposed nor free, which arrives at the betwixt time, neither night nor day, neither walking nor riding, and the poetry would be neither inside the house nor out.

1981, 1989

A PLAYFUL LOOK AT FORM

I.

The word "form" when used about any creation suggests the idea of shape or body. It is natural to ask then: When we talk of form in poetry, does that mean an intellectual body or a sensual body? I think most critics of poetry imagine form as an intellectual structure, or a mental skeleton. When one follows that view one concludes that form adds something hard to softness of feeling; it represents in small degree the eternal forms of which Plato speaks; it carries with it the clarity of the abstract or mathematical universe, the inexorable return of stars, the unemotional lines of geometry, the bony elegance of the triangle. I think there's much to be said for this concept of form and I don't intend to dismiss it.

Donald Hall however has laid out a contrasting view of what poetic form is, what meter and rhyme at base are, and he puts form's essence elsewhere. His idea is that form in poetry involves three kinds of fun (which he calls sensualities), all linked to the earliest weeks of our life. The first is the baby's enjoyment of sound, meaningless or not, which in the baby could be called mouth-fun or mouth-sensuality, and which in Milton becomes vast sonorities of vowels and consonants. The second sort of fun we see in the baby's kicking motions, especially when the baby is glad, and we could call that leg-fun or leg-sensuality, which continues as the adult's delight in dancing, and which informs those strong beats we notice in every line of Yeats. The third sort of fun is the infantile pleasure of appearance-disappearance. A baby sees its mother's face vanish, and loves to see it reappear again and vanish and reappear. That is very like the way the sound in a rhymed poem disappears, and then suddenly reappears again at the very last moment. Such sensuality could be called in the baby the pleasure of peek-a-boo or hiding and finding; and it becomes in adults the delight in rhyme and internal rhyme that we notice in every line of Marvell.

Donald Hall suggests that whenever we feel a given poem has "form," we are actually registering the presence of one or more of these forms of infantile fun. All three are easy to find in almost any Shakespearean sonnet. Here is mouth-sensuality or mouth-fun:

Bare ruined choirs where late the sweet birds sang

Here is kicking-fun or leg-stamping:

The expense of spirit in a waste of shame
Is lust in action, and till action, lust
Is perjured, murderous, bloody, full of blame,
Savage, extreme, rude, cruel, not to trust.

The sense of dance comes in through the alternate accents, and in Shakespeare's case probably in the tune to which most of the sonnets were sung. Here is the fun of peek-aboo experienced in rhymes and half-rhymes:

Shall I compare thee to a summer's day?
Thou are more lovely and more temperate;
Rough winds do shake the darling buds of May,
And summer's lease hath all too short a date . . .

In a Shakespeare sonnet the themes themselves perform an appearance-disappearance drama in the closing couplet as well, to the great delight of the mind.

II.

Hall gives a convincing demonstration that poetic form, when looked at impishly or playfully, does not relate itself only to adult discipline but to infantile pleasure as well. That assertion saws across the grain of a lot of wood. Many a poet defending himself from charges of doing nothing presents a picture of himself alone wrestling manfully with his craft hour after hour. His discipline in his craft is evidence surely of his serious adult attitude toward life.

To cavort with Hall's idea a little further, let's assume that the child-like and the infantile lie in the form; and the adult contribution lies in the meaning or content. Meaning and form then make two poles, across which the magnetic energy of the poem arches. Certain cheerful poets, whom I've called hoppers, bring the infantile into the content, and then there's no place for the adult grief to go. Other poets, who call themselves formalists, imagine their iambic meter is a kind of militaristic correction of Sixties sloppiness. When poets imagine form as adult, the meter becomes willed and mechanical; and what's worse is that there's no place now for the infantile spontaneity to go.

If, just for fun, we visualize the two poles of the poem in this new way — content as adult, form as child-like — we notice that they are opposites in their charge like the negative and positive poles of a battery. The cliché then that Charles Olson and many of his followers adopted, "Form is merely an extension of content," can be seen to be what it is — a ridiculous idea. It always was. Blake says that each artist needs the strength to endure the tension of fierce opposites. Blake's content is deeply adult, and his form deeply child-like and sensual. In his early poems particularly he is a child:

> Piping down the valleys wild,
> Piping songs of pleasant glee.

Poets and scholars, Pound among them, have pointed out the immense metrical and rhyming ingenuity involved in the composition of the troubadour poems. We know now that the Spanish and French troubadours were influenced in their poetry by the sensuality of Arab civilization, particularly Sufi religious sensibility, carried by images of erotic love. The aura of erotic pleasure shines out from the language body of these troubadour poems, and the fun is there, while in the content certain ascetic ideas about "the love from far away" are being spoken.

III.

There are two pulls. The playful form pulls the reader back toward infancy; the complicated meaning pulls the reader forward into adult states of mind. What happens when the poet places his or her most adult perceptions into the meaning? Then ascetic ideas (as in the Provençal poets) may come forward, compensating or contradicting the pleasure-loving language body; Heraclitean thought may come forward as in Machado, satire as in Quevedo, debate between Self and Soul as in Yeats, the praise of limits in Olaf Hauge or Tranströmer. The adolescent is aware of early wants and early losses; the adult is aware of great causes and mythological beings. The adult poem then has "responsibilities" (in the Yeats view), or character, which we could term the ability to absorb joyfully experiences carrying pain — an ability or responsibility the infant never dreams of in his crib.

Following Whitman, most contemporary poets have gone directly on an express bus to free verse. In the free verse that we write, child-like or adolescent perceptions make up the content, and a child-like honesty provides the tone of the simple form. I have often tried myself, especially in the *Snowy Fields* poems, for this double clarity. There is no crime in such simplicity, but it can be a form of denial — a way to keep away from certain areas of adult experience.

Keeping the poem's content child-like is understandable. American poets feel themselves surrounded by a prematurely senile, rigid and stiff-legged culture, and so they keep the garden of the poem for their adolescent impulses, their spontaneous fantasies.

Russian poets have remained closer to the old poetic forms than we have, or perhaps they struggle more with them. Voznesensky's appearance-disappearance in assonance and rhyme is spectacular. At the same time his content is adult, open to the anguish of the Russian situation. Emily Dickinson is "Russian" in that she never read Whitman. H.D.'s poems are impressive, particularly in the way the vowels are made to recur. Gerard Manley Hopkins is a genius ten times over in his mouth-sensuality, his leg-fun, and his appearance-disappearance.

Our contemporary free verse is so busy being democratic, expansive, clear and sincere, direct to the gut, that we lose the troubadours and other pre-Whitman ancestors. We need to have the wise religious crone back in content and the "wild old wicked man." How few poems in *The Best Poems of 1989*, a collection that I like, carry any hint of religious experience, neo-Platonic traditions, political agonies of choice, adult outrage, serious worship of Dionysius, debate on major issues. The Joseph Campbell interviews in his PBS series give a hint of what the wild old man and wise old crone content could be.

North American poetry in recent years continues to produce marvelous work from its best poets, poetry that is nourishing, lively, startling, and various; but in the matter of form-fun it is not so inventive. Playfully imaging complicated poetic form as infantile and child-like not only leaves a space open for adulthood in content, but allows us to think of form in a less academic way. Hall's idea loosens up the concept of form. His idea has something in it of Dionysius, "the Loosener."

1974-89

FORM IN SOCIETY AND IN THE POEM

I.

It seems that a feeling of constriction was habitual in the 19th century. To judge by literature, people felt a sense of constriction in the streets, in drawing rooms, and inside their heads. Jane Austen focused on it in the English country home; Dickens, in the streets. Rimbaud describes a thousand ways he felt restrained and hemmed in: he was suffocated by his boring town, the Alexandrine line, the stuffy subject matter, the stanza; he rebels against his family, the Second Empire, "ideas," literary society, and Europe. Such rebellion was a conjuring act that often took away the feeling of constriction, which was both political and literary. A rebel against certain forms in poetry was usually also a rebel against the aristocratic and bourgeois conventions. Whitman is a good example. He fought against the old poetic forms, bringing free verse, and also announced the end of class in society, the coming of brotherhood. The whole rebellious and iconoclastic tradition of the 19th century, continuing through Ibsen and Laforgue, emerges I think from this feeling of constriction, felt everyday in the consciousness.

In the 20th century we are half-conscious that too many babies are being born on earth, cities are expanding out of control, businesses join, publishers merge, corporations grow bigger and bigger. Even idea systems expand: industrialists become interested in Blacks and have liberal viewpoints, Continental Can supports Plato, old lefties work for *The National Review* — the living room of the mind widens to include other cultures, other galaxies. Everyone wants to be in a gaseous rather than a solid state. The Wall Street broker is troubled, like his peyote-chewing foil, by the expansion of his own ego, which seems nearly ready to fill the whole universe. This mood of uncontrollable expansion troubles us, just as its opposite, the mood of constriction, troubled those living in the 19th century.

II.

Our attitude toward expansion is ambiguous. The administration encourages expansion in business, but wants countries like Cuba to stay in their place. Ministers expand their churches, but dislike expansion in corporations. The American middle class senses an evil in expansion, but its attitude is confused. Allen Ginsberg, who is an intelligent man, embodies the expansion around him in his form, attacks it in his content, calling it "Moloch," and participates in it enthusiastically with his life.

That solution is characteristic: we feel troubled, but like the jazzy way of life and don't want to give it up. We end up praising it.

A person who praises what is destroying him can believe anything. We want to believe that American expansiveness is good, and so the most impossible thoughts on the subject of freedom and order are spoken and accepted. Many people have declared that drug use is freedom. Monopoly is free enterprise. Armies are for peace. The secretary of state says that Honduras is a part of the free world.

III.

In the nineteenth century the poet said, "Watch me. I have broken the forms in my poem, and the poetry remains. Do the same. Break the forms in community and the essence of community will remain." Rimbaud took this step, Whitman also. The essence of poetry remained when people broke forms, but the essence of community did not. In poetry, Yvor Winters and several contemporary followers advise us to reimpose old form. That may be all right. But we know from the experience of Germany and Italy in this century that modern society cannot be made livable by the reimposition of old forms.

Because the sense of constriction has come to an end, fruitful emphasis on freeing poetry from constriction has ended. All the work on overcoming constriction is no longer helpful, and critics in poetry and society are not agreed on how to approach expansion.

We know that some political leaders have been able to live out their infinite hungers by slipping past the old restraints of Parliament, custom, separation of powers, checks and balances. Hitler is an example — how easily he dissolved the German parliament. The so-called Savings and Loan scandal in the United States is another political example. The Congress removes "regulation" and instantly the owners of Savings and Loans fall into expansive grandiosity, and the loss expands to billions.

To return to the poem, we can say that the counting of beats in Anglo-Saxon poetry, the obligatory pause, the careful attention to opening consonants, the use of elaborate kennings and back references to old stories regulated and laid constraints on grandiosity. Poems that express opposing points of view, such as Yeats's "Dialogue of Self and Soul," amount to restraints on grandiosity; the purely lyric poem, by contrast — which expresses one point of view only — does not put any holds on infantile grandiosity. Milan Kundera complains that "the lyric poet always identifies himself with his feelings." From Kundera's point of view then, "the unbearable lightness of being" is precisely this lyrical expansionism, with no discrepancy between what things believe they are and what they are.

IV.

Something in us wants and wants endlessly. Witches and giants in fairy stories stand for that wanting. The witch wants a ton of wheat sorted in an hour, she wants all the fish in the river to be laid out by species and in neat rows this afternoon; the giant wants to eat now, now, now, and he can eat for days, he can eat all the food produced in the county this year. Goya's painting of Saturn eating his son suggests the anguish inseparable from that endless, repetitive, abusing hunger.

Kohut and the self psychologists have named the source of this infinite hunger infantile grandiosity or psychological omnipotence. When a two- or three-year-old child is on the grandiose road, it has godlike goals and is not at all sure that it is not God. Limits, conditions, bounds, confines are something the child doesn't want to hear of. Alice Miller remarks that each person chooses either the grandiose road or the depressed road; but, of course, inside each depressed person there is a grandiose person, and vice versa. It is infantile grandiosity that destroys the forests without counting the cost and pollutes the lakes. Longing for the infinite is at the root of American consumption of drugs, and policemen cannot help with that.

Whitman then is justly the American poet. He solved contradiction by expanding, and he did find the godlike. So Whitman is both authentically mystical and authentically infantile.

Our task here is not to point fingers, for the fingers would simply curve and point at us — author and reader alike — but to work toward an understanding of the grandiosity that has eroded both poetry and society in the twentieth century.

Side by side with the surrealist poetry of extreme lightness in the

United States is the poetry of flatness. Kohut's thought applies to this artistic problem. He believes that the godlike omnipotence inside the adult person, preserved from early childhood, troubles him or her; its omnipotence, even though curtailed and driven back by parents, schoolmates, driving instructors, and priests, remains inside, cooking. The omnipotence has an open channel, never broken, to the infinite heat of God's room, which we can imagine as the Castle of Stromberg, the White Bear's mansion, the realm of archetypes, or the reaction chambers of the physical sun. Some people who are terrified of grandiosity spend their vital energy defending themselves from the godlike furnace cooking inside them. They are the flat people. Side by side with the light poetry we have the flat poetry of the universities, flatter than any poetry ever known in the world before. In the first the poet gives association haphazardly, and ascends out of sight; in the second the poet resists association, sticks to the facts, and receives his certificate in genuine nongrandiosity.

Providing associative poetry without emotional content is a technique of the ascenders; reimposing traditional meter is a technique of the flat people. Neither should be rejected, but there must be a third way. It lies in a poetry that keeps its connection to wildness, to grandiosity, and to mythological magnificence, and at the same time builds into the lines the planned pitches, the pauses, the sound-repetitions that the Anglo-Saxon poets used to support and regulate their wildness. The subject to some degree would be grandiosity itself. And the rhythms would be depressed. Limits enter in that way. The mood would be proper to our failures. Then the poet could say to society: "I have broken my grandiosity, and the essence of the human remains."

1961, 1990

PRAISING THE SEVEN HOLY VOWELS

I.

There are so many pleasures in poetry, even in slices of a poem. Sometimes thought in a poem curls back on itself, so swiftly! It flies. For entomologists, every square meter has to be exhaustively investigated for resident beetles and old varieties of fire ants, but in poetry we have the pleasure of circulating. What's important is the wind going through your feathers. Wallace Stevens once said:

> Remus, blow your horn!
> I'm ploughing on Sunday,
> Ploughing North America.
> Blow your horn!
>
> Tum-ti-tum,
> Ti-tum-tum-tum!
> The turkey-cock's tail
> Spreads to the sun.
>
> The white cock's tail
> Streams to the moon.
> Water in the fields.
> The wind pours down.
>
> ("Ploughing on Sunday")

We're going to talk here about the high spirits that lie in the music of sounds—a music created by a cunning repeating or chiming of small sounds. Wallace Stevens is a genius at that too. Here is the first stanza of his poem on a dying lady:

> A lady dying of diabetes
> Listened to the radio,
> Catching the lesser dithyrambs.
> So heaven collects its bleating lambs.

We notice first the rhyme of "dithyrambs" with "lambs." But returning to the opening couplet, we can see brilliant repeating of the *ee* sound in the first line with "diabetes." "Dying of diabetes" includes two *ai* sounds. How important the second *ai* sound is we realize if we try to substitute another word: "A lady dying of tuberculosis" is terrible; "A lady dying of bronchial pneumonia" or "A lady dying of cirrhosis" becomes, strangely, prose. We need "diabetes" for its *ee* sound so it can resonate with the *ee* in "lady."

> A lady dying of diabetes
> Listened to the radio.

Also we notice that the *ee* sound resonates with the *ee* in lady and with the middle vowel of "radio." The *s* of "listened" responds to the *s* of "diabetes"; and the *ay* in "radio" catches the *ay* of "lady."

> A lady dying of diabetes
> Listened to the radio,
> Catching the lesser dithyrambs.
> So heaven collects its bleating lambs.

We have been hearing the dance of sounds. If a poet doesn't provide for the interior chimings of sounds, we still understand the thought perhaps, but we will have missed a major pleasure.

One notices that the word "so" at the start of the fourth line has caught and amplified the *oh* of "radio." This chiming of sounds resembles an amplifier in technological life. The word "bleating" amplifies the *ee* sounds of the first two lines. So one has to say that this first stanza is perfect in its pleasures, magnificent. His concentration on this old dying lady continues as follows:

> Her useless bracelets fondly fluttered,
> Paddling the melodic swirls,
> The idea of god no longer sputtered.
> At the roots of her indifferent curls.
>
> The idea of the Alps grew large,
> Not yet, however, a thing to die in.

It seemed serener just to die,
To float off on the floweriest barge,

Accompanied by the exegesis
Of familiar things in a cheerful voice,
Like the night before Christmas and all the carols.
Dying lady, rejoice, rejoice!

(from "The Mechanical Optimist")

The reader can follow, without a lot of guidance, the elaborate dance of sounds going on in these final three stanzas. We can pick out the sound particles: *er* is amplifying itself with "longer," "her," "curls," "serener"; and *in* is amplifying itself with "paddling," "indifferent," "thing," "die in," etc. Stevens never loses track of *ee,* and his unusual word "exegesis" is a big amplifier. The final line—which is so marvelous—

Dying lady, rejoice, rejoice!

gives us *ee* three times, and closes the poem with a major vowel. The poem then, as a musical composition, closes as any good piece by Mozart might, with a burst of gorgeous, understated, precise, cunningly elaborated, joyful sounds.

2.

We might say a few words about the Seven Holy Vowels. Joscelyn Godwin, in *The Mystery of the Seven Vowels,* has written a lively history of the speculations that the Egyptians, the classical Greeks, the Hebrews, the Pythagoreans, the Muslims, the Celts brought forward about the vowels in ancient times, as well as the more recent speculations by G. R. S. Mead, H. P. Blavatsky, and Rimbaud. Most ancient speculations suggest that the main seven vowels symbolize "the primary sounds emitted by the seven heavenly bodies." The long *oh* as in *holy* is the sound of Saturn; *oo* is the sound of Jupiter, the short *o* is Mars, *ai* is the sun, long *ee* is Venus, short *e* is Mercury, *ay* is the moon.

We recall that Rimbaud found it valuable to assign colors to each of the major vowels, indicating how seriously he took their possibilities for communication. There is no absolute agreement on the relationship of the colors to the vowels, and so it's perfectly permissible for each of us to make these sounds at great length in our rooms and then ask our body what color she prefers. For *ah,* which Rimbaud associated with the caverns of the mouth, he preferred black; the long *e,* as in *see,* he felt was scarlet merging toward purple; the long *oh,* as in *holy,* he felt to be the deep blue of the sky.

The power of the seven main vowels has stirred human beings as far back in time as we can peek. One idea is that each major vowel affects the physical body; and the body responds by trying to move in a certain way. When the body hears a certain vowel, for example, it may want to lift the arms and enclose something.

Finally, we might mention the possibility that each vowel can be associated fruitfully with one of the notes in our typical musical scale. Such a possibility would give a poet twenty-five years of wonderful study.

3.

The Seven Holy Vowels that we'll look at will be these seven: *ay* as in *hay, ee* as in *see, ai* as in *sky, oh* as in *bold, oo* as in *you, ah* as in *father,* and *ohm* as in *home.* It's possible that we have been responding physically to these vowels since we were in the womb. *The Secret Life of the Unborn Child* by Thomas Verny, for example, provides evidence, some gained by ultrasound experiments, that babies in the womb respond very much to sound. Babies love single-melody Bach, as on a cello or piano, but they don't care for orchestral Bach. They seem to love all of Mozart. They hate rock music and tend to shrink up when they hear it. They are equally alert to language. Babies show a different response to a noun than to a verb. Some respond even to prepositions. That means of course that they are not only bathed in fluid during their nine months but in sound.

Donald Hall, in his essay "Goatfoot Milktongue Twinbird," connects the pleasures of poetry, one might say the deliciousness of sound in poetry, with mouth pleasure after birth. He calls the mouthing of vowels "milktongue," as if our love of poetry began while nursing and continues into adult life, keeping the form of great sensual joy at the nipple. If the poet doesn't open his or her mouth wide enough at poetry readings, Don will accuse the poet of mouth-guilt. Several times he has accused me of this fault, which is not really a fault, but a simple characteristic of Midwestern farmers. It's clear from all this that Dylan Thomas was an exuberant vowel and nipple lover. We're getting distracted here; and we need to return to the idea that when a vowel is spoken slowly the body attempts to respond.

We could start with the vowel *oh*. The body seems to know what it wants to do. If you want to try your body out with this, stand up, and speak the sound *oh* loudly for a while, then stretch your arms out to each side. Some people find that as they keep on making the sound *oh*, their two arms move slowly toward each other, enclosing something invisible until finally the fingers touch and sometimes interlock. The sound *oh*, then, apparently makes the body long for enclosure, devotion, holding, all of which we sometimes feel in the word "holy."

We won't go over here each of the seven vowel sounds; but we might mention *ah*. In many cultures *ah* is felt to be the strongest vowel of them all. We notice it appears once in our word "God," but twice in the Muslim word "Allah." The body seems to respond to *ah* by longing to lift its arms above the head toward the sun and stars. You might try saying *ah* for a long time and see what happens. The *oo* sound seems to have to do with intimacy, as in "moon" and "you." Sometimes when a man or woman speaks softly the sound *oo*, arms remain at the side for a while and then come slowly up on each side of the face; sometimes the thumbs go underneath the chin and the spread fingers frame or protect the intimacy of the face. Goethe loved the sound *oo*, and in the German of his great poem "Wanderers Nachtlied II" he repeats the sound *oo* five times in eight or so lines. The poem ends:

> Warte nur, balde
> Ruhest du auch.

There is something delicious about playing with these seven vowels and noticing how one's own body wants to respond to them. The chiming of sounds in poetry, then, appeals to the ear in what we call the joy of music, but also each large sound or holy vowel activates the body in a pleasurable way. Of course we now speak so fast that the body doesn't have a chance to give its response.

4.

Those of us who want to pursue this matter farther can learn by heart and chant Yeats's early poem called "The Lake Isle of Innisfree." The poem opens with the line:

I will arise and go now, and go to Innisfree.

That line has a total of 13 syllables, five of which are long vowels. The poem is an amazing accomplishment in sound; and we know that after Yeats published that poem, he received several letters from professors of literature at Irish universities who said they'd never known what a vowel was before they spoke that poem.

I will arise and go now, and go to Innisfree,
And a small cabin build there, of clay and wattles made:
Nine bean-rows will I have there, a hive for the honey-bee,
And live alone in the bee-loud glade.

In much poetry the live limbs of the lines, so to speak, reside utterly in the long vowels. You can hear a Farsi speaker reciting Rumi today, and you will hear a sequence of short and long vowels which become a kind of dance. The long vowels, as we can understand from the Yeats line, call for chanting. Ancient Greek meter is much like that; Sappho and Alcaeus developed different patterns of long and short vowels which were so satisfying that poets used them for centuries. Statius, for example, the third century Latin poet, wrote most of his great poems in the meter that Alcaeus developed for Greek. In our century, Tomas Tranströmer has written three poems in Swedish which follow precisely the same meter of Alcaeus.

In English, we have an immense number of short vowels in comparison to the number of long vowels, so that it's very difficult to use long vowels as the root of the meter. There's always a feeling of strain when a poet in English asks for a number of long vowels. There just aren't enough of them. We can feel that strain in Gerard Manley Hopkins. Because of that shortage of long vowels, most English poets have to make do with a meter such as iambic, based on beats or accents, in which the long vowels come in at the rate of two long vowels for each ten syllables roughly, but no more. So we get moderate pleasure in sound, but probably not as much pleasure as Iranian singers do when they speak or sing the Farsi of Rumi.

5.

To close this little essay about the pleasures that sounds give in poetry, we're going to move now to a consideration of sound that's more congenial to the English language, with its enormous number of prepositions and tiny words like *and* and *the*, and the many words in English that sometimes, like *invisibility* or *determinism*, have no long vowels in them at all. We'll return to those strange units such as *in* and *ar* and *an* and *or* that contain in themselves so much music, the units that the language experts, who have very little sense of language, call phonemes. We'll call these things sound particles. They are really little creatures—*in* and *am* and *el* and *il* and *en*. Grasping these little sounds with the pincers of our ears is a more exciting process in English than it is in some other languages, because English provides so many weird multiple spellings for any one of these sound particles. The *ir* in "bird," for example, we also find in "Byrd" and "burr," even in "world." A sound particle amounts to the union of a small vowel and a consonant, the one leaning on the other, so to speak, two friends who are never parted, who always sing the same little tune, no matter how it's spelled.

No one knows how many sound particles there are. In the Deep South, strange sound particles flow out of the mouth using vowels that never pass New England lips. So we can't be too picky about how many sound particles there are in the English language. Most people write some poetry—it's interesting to look over your own poems and see which sound particles you seem to prefer. That tells a lot about the tunes that come off your personality. There's a great deal of pleasure around sound particles in Robert Lowell's first book, called *Lord Weary's Castle.* He loved particularly *ar* and *in.* Here are the first five lines of "The Holy Innocents":

> Listen, the hay-bells tinkle as the cart
> Wavers on rubber tires along the tar
> And cindered ice below the burlap mill
> And ale-wife run. The oxen drool and start
> In wonder at the fenders of a car . . . .

You can see he's stretching things a little here and there in order to get "car," "cart," "tar," and "start" in one stanza, but it works. He also brings in related sound particles in "tire" and "burlap" and "drool." Among particles related to *in* he pulls in "run," "oxen," "wonder," "fender," and so on. Finally it all seems right, or nearly right, because we are being fed at some deep level.

I'm very fond of *in* myself and its relatives *er* and *ern,* as well as the sound particle *ir,* which also has its connection in *ern.* I wrote a little love poem which goes this way:

> It was among ferns I learned about eternity.
> Below your belly there's a curly place.
> Through you I learned to love the ferns on that bank,
> And the curve the deer's hoof leaves in sand.

The *n* sounds appear in *among, learned, ferns, eternity, learned, ferns, bank,* and, *sand.* The *ir* sound particle appears in *fern, learn, eternity, curly, learned, ferns, curve,* along with its companion sound particles *or* in *your, air* in *there,* and *ear* in *deer.* You notice that the *ir* sound particle appears three times in the opening line, and we notice that it makes a change in the word *eternity* when it is the third in the sequence.

There are so many pleasures in poetry—some from playfulness, some from intensity of feeling, some from swiftness of thought. To me the greatest pleasure arrives from the intentful chiming of sounds, from worship of the sound particles and the Seven Holy Vowels.

THE LONG VOWELS

I.

Whenever we talk of human life, we are talking about participation and separation. Each of us lives much of our time in separation, but in poetry we can each imagine various ways in which we move from separation to participation.

A great image by its very nature can increase participation. Georg Trakl ended a poem "On Golgotha God's eyes slowly open." In the sensual immersion of the image we are reminded that the trees and the animals and the dark are near us; at the same time, every metaphor implies that some separation has already taken place, or we wouldn't move to bring things back together. Psychic weight is that, we could also say, in which participation increases; by psychic weight, a certain feeling of grief as the human being acknowledges limitations and settles down to the grief that the badger and the porcupine live in all the time. We'd probably all agree that psychic weight and the sensual image contribute to participation, but I want to say now that it is sound and only sound that holds the secret of participation in poetry. One who loves sounds repeats sounds and asks them to call to each other, but only, of course, if the sound is the right sound, the just one, the sound the early human who knew participation well would use. So the first power of this area of poetry is the power of the word—the word before it is separated, not so much from its "thing" but from the motion of the wind, what the Chinese call the *tao*, before it is separated from the body's own motion.

2.

We are thinking of sound here not only as that vocal act which contributes to meaning, to denotation, and so affects the mind of others. We are thinking of sound here more as a vibratory pattern that wants to move the body in a certain way. Every time we hear a sound clearly some part of our body wakes up, wants to lift the arms or turn the head or widen the chest. This whole tradition that tries to understand how bodies are activated, made more alive by sound, is associated with the tradition of what Jocelyn Godwin calls the Seven Holy Vowels.

The power of spoken vowels has stirred human beings as far back into time as we can peek. The gods themselves often have names composed only of vowels. For example, there was an old god named Iao, which in our sound system we would probably spell out as *ai-ah-oh*. Abbé Barthelemy mentions that this name often appears with images of Harpocrates, the child god of the winter solstice. The long vowel *ai* corresponds to the Sun. As for *ah* and *oh,* they are *alpha* and *omega, ay* and *oh,* the first and last letters of the Greek alphabet, so that the name *Iao* could mean the *Sun Which Begins and Ends All Things.*

Let's talk a moment about the Mystery or occult interpretation of sound. There is a common-sense understanding of sound for people who wish to know no more, and then there is the hidden or Orphic or Mystery School point of view, for those who want to remember their connections to the invisible world.

In the twelfth book of the *Odyssey,* Odysseus and his sailors approach certain bird-headed women whose cries tend to make sailors leap off the ship, particularly sailors who are not initiated. Odysseus tells the rowers to put beeswax in their ears; if anyone wants to listen, his friends should tie him to the mast. From the Mystery School point of view, the sounds the bird-headed women make remind the soul of the place from which the soul arrived here. We all know that home can be reached again only by the sacrifice of the material body. The emphasis then is not on men being tied so that they are going to live but men who are tied so that their bodies cannot respond to the meaning of the sounds that they hear. It is much like the way we tie ourselves to a television set so that the flood of pictures prevents us from hearing the sounds inside the words being spoken. One could say that the constant cacophany of boomboxes and muzak have been instituted particularly to prevent us from hearing healthful and ecstatic sounds from the other world.

Now we want to come down into the physical world and simply examine these seven vowels. There is again no universal decision which seven vowels are the primary ones. Every culture has in some way that is hard to understand a different shaped mouth, and so the sounds are amazingly different in German, for example, from French. It drives the sound scholars mad. We will ignore all that and talk of the seven vowels as our mouths make them. For our purposes, the seven we'll adopt are as follows: *ay* as in *hay, e* as in *see, ai* as in *sky, oh* as in *bold, oo* as in *you, ah* as in *father,* and *ohm* as in *home.*

We'll return for a moment to the old concept that each of the sounds makes our body want to respond in a certain way with a certain motion, using certain limbs.

Let's try *ay*. Many people, when they say *ay* over and over, find their arms going straight out to the side, sometimes with the forearms vertical, making a kind of cup shape. The one for *e* is very funny. There's tremendous energy for *e*, as you can feel in your body when you say *e*. Some people feel it's connected with determination and honor and vitality. So for some, *e* means that the arms hang down and then you lift the forearms until they're parallel to the floor, then you raise them up toward your shoulders in a kind of pumping motion. With *ai*, one of the favorite positions is to have the arms straight up above the head, drop the palms slightly, and it has to do with laughter and gaiety. Dorothy Parker probably kept her hands above her head like this. You'll see sometimes film of an entire audience in the Sixties greeting the Doors with this gesture. With *oh*, almost everyone agrees on the typical gesture the body wants to make. Put your arms out to the side, and then the longer you make the sound, the more the arms come toward each other until finally the fingers interlock. The sound seems to be associated with trust and kindness, as in the word *holy*. The long *oo* was one of Goethe's favorite sounds, and I'll speak a poem of his here. In English, one translation of the poem might go:

On the tops of the hills
There is silence.
In the tops of the trees
You feel
Hardly a breath.
The little birds fall silent in the trees.
Simply wait: Soon
You too will be silent.

But in German it says:

Über allen Gipfeln
Ist Ruh,
In allen Wipfeln
Spürest du

Kaum einen Hauch;
Die Vögelein schweigen im Walde.
Warte nur, balde
Ruhest du auch.

The *oo* sound seems to have to do with loyalty, with closeness, devotion and a kind of release. We could say that Goethe, when he was in the woods at sunset, felt a deep participation between his body and the woods, because his body like the birds understood that night was coming and by extension they were going to die. Since Goethe does not hate this participation, it is also a release.

The sound *ah* is usually done with the arms upward and forward and seems to be associated with joy, particularly the joy of discipline, with justice, and harmony. That's probably why it is in the baby's sound *ma* and *pa, mama* and *papa,* and so there is something religious in the sound. We notice that that is the sound we have in God. One of the reasons that the Muslims threw us out of the Holy Land is that their God had it twice, *Allah.* How could we stand up to two *ahs*? In some traditions, the palms are turned to face our own face.

The strangest one is the sound for *ohm.* It's fairly old, the legs apart and the arms at about a forty-five degree angle, so that with the head it makes a five-pointed star. It seems to be associated with mystery, possibly the mystery of birth itself, possibly the security in the womb, possibly the human body as a place which simultaneously lives in the invisible world as well as in the physical world. And the famous sound pattern of the Tibetans, sometimes spoken several thousand times a day in a monastery for the good of all living people, goes in the Tibetan pronunciation *ohm man-nee pay-ma hmm.* So you could say that they brought five of the major seven vowels into this one, *ohm,* and then the long *ah* in *man,* the long *ee* in *nee,* then the long *ay* in *pay* and then another long *ah* in *pay-ma hmm.* And the *hmm* is actually in some traditions spoken in a fierce way as to keep the demons away while we perform these seven vowels.

3.

It's clear now that by vowels, we mean long vowels. By holy vowels, we refer to the ones the voice can lengthen out. There are many minor vowels, but they usually become attached to the consonant on either side.

We're going to talk next of vowels as a part of what we might call a private meter. We'll take as a text Yeats's poem called "Her Dream," which is actually his dream. After years of his enforced chastity, in order to be romantically true to his great love, Maud Gonne, he had a dream. In the dream, Maud was dead, and he saw her gravestone. He cut off a piece of his hair and put it on the gravestone. Suddenly an enormous eagle flew down, snatched up the hair, and disappeared into the night sky, where the hair became a part of the constellation called Berenice's Hair. This is what he did with it:

I dreamed as in my bed I lay,
All night's fathomless wisdom come,
That I had shorn my locks away
And laid them on Love's lettered tomb;
But something bore them out of sight
In a great tumult of the air,
And after nailed upon the night
Berenice's burning hair.

This poem in its outward or public meter is a four-beat iambic line. That becomes clear in standard lines such as "That I had shorn my locks away," "but something bore them out of sight" and "And after nailed upon the night." But as we look at the more problematic lines, "All night's fathomless wisdom come," "And laid them on Love's lettered tomb," "In a great tumult of the air," it's clear that some powerful energy is coming up from beneath and disturbing the even flow of the iambic water. That energy is vowel energy. Or one could say that the poem has two meters, one public and one private, and the two meters are wrestling with each other, causing a lot of disturbance.

The private meter we can only grasp if we are willing to speak the poem and not speak it but chant it, and chant it in a way that lengthens out some of the vowels, in a way to a degree no longer done in poetry recital. I'll recite the poem as it proceeds along its private or inward road, and we'll see that it is basically not a four-beat line but a two-vowel line:

I *dreamed* as in my bed I *lay*,

All night's *fathom*less wisdom *come,*
That I had *shorn* my locks *away*
And *laid* them on Love's lettered *tomb;*
But something *bore* them out of *sight*
In a *great tum*ult of the air,
And after *nailed* upon the *night*
Bere*nice's* burning *hair.*

We'll see at times that there are third vowels that keep surfacing such as "locks" and "Love's" and "some" and "air" and probably "burn" from "burning." Sometimes, depending on our mood, one vowel or another will surface instead of the other to express the voice's urgencies, but in general we have here lines with eight syllables and, when spoken, two holy vowels. Typically for Yeats, he raises the sound particles *orn* or *bore* up and turns them into long vowels. With the Irish *r* and given a slow day, it probably took him two or three minutes to pronounce *shorn.*

4.

The last question we want to ask about long vowels is what long vowels can do in an ordinary line. In Yeats they become part of a structure, but they can appear also in ordinary poems. It's clear that a long vowel is a carrier for intense emotion, and the soul itself is somehow related to the intense, expanding sound that a long vowel provides for. But the long vowel also gives the mind a sense of conviction that what has just been said is true, and that it represents the deepest thought of the poet. Robert Frost in talking about how the dust in San Francisco as a child had an influence on his whole life, ends his poem this way:

I was one of the children told
Some of the blowing dust was gold.

He has one *oh* in the first line and two in the second line, and something very satisfying comes in with these long vowels. *I* is a long vowel. It's as if there's a pause after *I* that we can't see. "*I* was one of the children *told.*" It's another line with eight syllables but two long vowels. After *told,* there's another pause, impossible to account for. It looks almost like this:

I was one of the children *told*
(Wing-wing) *Some* of the *blowing* dust was *gold.*

So our point here is that the careful use of long vowels has an unexpected influence on the time. It's as if it produces extra time within the line, as in those days when happiness brings you three or four extra minutes that others do not experience. We know that much ancient poetry, in Greek and in Farsi, for example, uses the long vowel as the entire base for the meter. In Farsi then, and in Greek, the poet uses the private meter and not the public one at all.

In English we don't have enough long vowels in comparison to the number of short vowels, so we are doomed to write in a public meter, such as iambic, which is based on beats or accents, "That time of year thou may'st in me behold," or "Shall I compare thee to a summer's day?" Whenever a genius such as Shakespeare uses the public meter, one can always feel the private meter underneath trying to break through. Shakespeare's early sonnets are amazingly interesting in that respect. All the evidence is that they, like some of the Italian sonnets, were written to a tune, the word *sonnet* being obviously connected to *sonata.* I found one day a tune still used in the Anglican church which fits all of the early Shakespeare sonnets, in which almost without exception the fourth syllable and the tenth syllable are long vowels. One should say that Shakespeare gives, since the providing of long vowels to the ear is always a gift, long vowels to whoever happens to be inhabiting the fourth place in line and the tenth place. An example would be the one we have already started. We'll place bold for the vowels in the fourth and tenth places that are long, and as we sing it, it will be absolutely clear how the private meter is coming forward.

Shall I com**pare** thee to a summer's **day**?
Thou art more **love**ly and more temper**ate:**
Rough winds do **shake** the darling buds of **May**,
And summer's **lease** hath all too short a **date:**

Sometime too **hot** the eye of heaven **shines**,
And often **is** his gold complexion **dimm'd**;
And every **fair** from fair sometime de**clines**,
By chance, or **na**ture's changing course, un**trimm'd**;

But thy e**ter**nal summer shall not **fade**,
Nor lose pos**ses**sion of that fair thou **ow'st**;
Nor shall death **brag** thou wander'st in his **shade**,
When in e**ter**nal lines to time thou **grow'st**:

So long as **men** can breathe or eyes can **see**
So long lives **this**, and this gives life to **thee**.

I'll sing it for you now. So it's clear from this little song that the long vowel, the holy vowel, gives the voice a place to rest, just as the garden gives the soul a place to rest, and the body and the soul appreciate it tremendously, particularly if they can look forward in the next line to one place to rest, or even better, two. If we have lost touch with the old tradition of carefully implanted long vowels, then our poems are liable to be, as we expect them to be, places where we bounce on and on, and we get somewhere, but there were no inns, and when we finish the poem we don't feel satisfied, and we don't feel rested.

1995

A WEEK OF GHAZALS

"The Night Abraham Called to the Stars"

The poems that you'll see this week will be unfamiliar in several ways. These new poems are modeled on a form called the ghazal; it began as a love poem in Arabic in the 10th century, and the word actually means "love poem." Since that, the subject matter has broadened, and the ghazal has become the major poetic form in a number of languages such as Urdu, Farsi, and Hindi.

This first poem mentions a story about Abraham that is remembered in the Qur-an. Both the Qur-an and the Old Testament have many stories about Abraham, which most of us know. The Qur-an includes his dismay when he watched the moving stars set. We could say that sometime in the very far past there was a moment in which human beings realized that the planets were not God. The Qur-an gives this moment to Abraham. The poem sympathizes with Abraham, but still contains admiration for the setting stars.

We could say that some people—they are usually called saints—love the eternal stars. Many other people don't care about religion at all. I am somewhere in between: I still love the setting stars. I suppose the setting stars are a little like bootleggers, and classmates who stole things once in a while, and reckless people like my friend Alte Clemenson who always shot pheasants out of season.

Quite a few of us—probably men and women born on farms—have badger souls. Muddy fields are OK; digging in the ground for potatoes is OK; big overshoes are OK; dragging mud into the house is OK. We are not really fitted for city life; we have to go back to lakes or farms every once in a while. Luckily many people in my family have continued farming, so I'm not too far from the muddy shoes or the smell of wet sheep, and I can go to the Minnesota State Fair to see the big hogs.

There's a potato in the last stanza. I'm not sure how it got there, maybe because of all my thinking about digging. My wife was very surprised when she realized I had called my heart a potato— "A potato?" "Well," I said, "a calm potato." "That's a little better," she said. But in my heart there is also a sorrowful woman, that I don't talk about very much. "Friends, tell me what to do, since I am a man in love with the setting stars."

The Night Abraham Called to the Stars

Do you remember the night Abraham first called
To the stars? He cried to Saturn: "You are my Lord!"
How happy he was! When he saw the Dawn Star,

He cried, "You are my Lord!" How destroyed he was
When he watched them set. Friends, he is like us:
We take as our Lord the stars that go down.

We are faithful companions to the unfaithful stars.
We are diggers, like badgers; we love to feel
The dirt flying out from behind our back claws.

And no one can convince us that mud is not
Beautiful. It is our badger soul that thinks so.
We are ready to spend the rest of our life

Walking with muddy shoes in the wet fields.
We resemble exiles in the kingdom of the serpent.
We stand in the onion fields looking up at the night.

My heart is a calm potato by day, and a weeping
Abandoned woman by night. Friend, tell me what to do,
Since I am a man in love with the setting stars.

"Rembrandt's Portrait of Titus with a Red Hat"

I began this poem in London one day when I visited a small museum called The Wallace Collection and saw there one of the five or six portraits that Rembrandt did of his son Titus. In this particular portrait Titus seems to be about 15 and is wearing a red velvet cap. Rembrandt always decided in every painting from which direction the light was coming, and then he knew where the shadows would be. He seems to have loved the shadows as much as the face.

> It's enough for light to fall on one half of a face.
> Let the other half belong to the restful shadow. . . .

In the second stanza I'm still thinking about the light that comes down from above in Rembrandt's paintings. The horse stalls in a barn are often dusky; sometimes during the day, sunlight will come down through a crack in the hayloft floor. I remember that light very well from my childhood.

The Dutch were a little disturbed about how much Rembrandt liked brown. As he got older, that increased; more and more black came in toward the edges of his paintings, as if it were advancing in from the world. He may be right: Maybe using a lot of bright and cheerful colors is a way to lie about life. Maybe the artist needs some place inside his own painting where he or she can be safe from too much observation.

In the next stanza I go back to Titus and particularly to his eyes. His face is very trusting, and yet the eyes have some doubt in them, as if he were puzzled about so many sudden disappearances in this world.

I have always been fond of Rembrandt's paintings and etchings that describe Mary and Joseph on the way to Egypt. Rembrandt usually shows them at night with Mary riding a donkey. We remember Herod's rage at the possibility of a holy boy somewhere in his territory. Perhaps Rembrandt felt some fear that Titus might be in danger, and darkness probably felt like protection to Rembrandt. Water soaked in onions produces a soft and generous color, and I imagine Rembrandt protecting his son by washing him in that water.

Rembrandt's Portrait of Titus with a Red Hat

It's enough for light to fall on one half of a face.
Let the other half belong to the restful shadow,
The shadow the bowl of bread throws on the altar.

Some paintings are like a horse's eating place
At the back of the barn where a single beam
Of light comes down from a crack in the ceiling.

Painting bright colors may lie about the world.
Too many windows cause the artist to hide.
Too many well-lit necks call for the axe.

Beneath his red hat, Titus's eyes hint to us
How puzzled he is by the sweetness of the world—
The way the dragonfly hurries to its death.

So many forces want to kill the young
Male who has been blessed. The Holy Family
Has to hide many times on the way to Egypt.

Titus receives a scattering of darkness.
He's baptized by water soaked in onions;
The father protects his son by washing him in the night.

"The Eel in the Cave"

When we are young, we hope for the best, and overlook our own faults, hoping others will do likewise. But at seventy, one gives up that plan. There's too much evidence. Each of us at seventy know that we probably belong in court.

I found copies recently of letters I had written to my mother when I was living a garret life in New York in my twenties. I felt something eerie in them, as if a man older than I was at the time had written them. Many people have experiences like that. It's as if someone inside us—whom we haven't entirely met—has already understood the disastrous or glad directions our life would take.

"Why is it our fault if we fall into desire?" reminds me how frequently we use the word "fall." We don't say, "I've enjoyed bad company," but "I fell into bad company." We don't say "I rose in love" but "I fell in love." This image of the falling that turns out well reminds us of the *felix culpa,* or "happy crime," by which many Catholic theologians refer to the mistake Adam and Eve made in the Garden. Many traditions say as well that each soul has chosen to come here, and so has chosen a fall down to this earth. The reason why the soul does that is not clear. Blake says the soul loves water. I give as a reason that the soul is attracted by those eels in mysterious undersea caves.

I am always aware how close I've come to dying in my life. I remember falling out of a car when I was two and watching the old Model A go down the road. So many men my age died in the Second World War; I was probably saved by rheumatic fever I caught in the Navy. Many of us have also fallen into depressions that we were lucky to get out of. Escaping from depression at times feels like a blessing.

A couple of years ago my wife and I visited the Alhambra, that amazing architectural masterpiece left behind by the Moors in Grenada. In the last line of the poem I mention that even though I do not deserve it, I am sometimes allowed to slip into that castle by night.

The Eel in the Cave

Our veins are open to shadow, and our fingertips
Porous to murder. It's only the inattention
Of the prosecutors that lets us go to lunch.

Reading my old letters I notice a secret will.
It's as if another person had planned my life.
Even in the dark, someone is hitching the horses.

That doesn't mean I have done things well.
I have found so many ways to disgrace
Myself, and throw a dark cloth over my head.

Why is it our fault if we fall into desire?
The eel poking his head from his undersea cave
Entices the tiny soul falling out of Heaven.

So many invisible angels work to keep
Us from drowning; so many hands reach
Down to pull the swimmer from the water.

Even though the District Attorney keeps me
Well in mind, grace allows me sometimes
To slip into the Alhambra by night.

"The Wagon and the Cliff"

Most of us are fond of Emerson, but he had a maddening tendency to say that everything is all right in the universe:

> Even the corpse that has lain in the chambers has added a solemn ornament to the house. The soul will not know either deformity or pain. . . . All loss, all pain, is particular; the universe remains to the heart unhurt. Neither vexations nor calamities abate our trust. No man ever stated his griefs as lightly as he might. (from "Spiritual Laws")

He wrote this when he was about thirty. Enough shocks happened to him later to make him doubt his own optimism. I just added a couple more.

Many people of optimistic turn of mind are tempted to say that no one is really greedy. I think the opposite. I think people are greedy and also badgers, swans, lions, peacocks and crows. Any one of them would probably agree to carry a just man to prison if there were anything in it for them.

In Greek mythology, Hippolytus, whose name suggest his connection with horses, was famous for his puritanism and his dislike of all romance. Aphrodite hates that sort of thing, and she decided to settle the matter. She got the Lord of the Sea to take care of him. One day when Hippolytus was driving his horses along the stony beach, the Lord of the Sea rose with larger horses than his. That frightened his horses, who then broke his chariot and pulled him along the stones until he died.

The mourning dove's call is so beautiful. When I was a boy on the farm, we could hear that delicate coo as soon as we woke in the morning. But doves want what they want. They want their territory; and they'll smash eggs in other mourning doves' nests if that neighbor is too close.

Many of us have seen the passport photos of our immigrant ancestors, which often shows what these people look like when they left Norway. My great-grandfather Helge and his wife Guri carry a massive unhappiness in their shoulder and neck, and their faces seem to express the pain that comes from too little food as a child, from anger against neighbors, the sadness of endless work. How could it have been otherwise? If they had been happy, they would have stayed where they were and not have come over here to a sod hut.

One requirement of the ghazal that is not always fulfilled by modern or ancient writers is that the writer is asked in the last stanza of the ghazal to step into the light so the reader can see how he fits into everything that has gone before. I had to notice that in my early poems I often expressed an optimism similar to Emerson's, such as, "Oh on an early morning I think I shall live forever." That optimistic mood is not a part of these Abraham poems. I don't think it's wrong that my old light-heartedness is gone; in fact, I like the "smoke of sadness" that has slipped into these poems.

The Wagon and the Cliff

The pin fails, and the wagon goes over the cliff.
The doctor steps out a moment and the boy dies.
We might question Emerson about this moment.

Please don't imagine that only people are greedy.
When a crow lifts off, its ungainly wings
Can carry a thousand Mandelas to the Island.

Hippolytus resisted women a little too much
And the Lady of the Sea decided against him.
His horses agreed to drag him along the stones.

Mourning doves singing from the fenceposts
When I was a boy woke the whole countryside.
But a dove's breastbone is a cathedral of desire.

Sometimes the saints make us seem better than we are.
Our ancestors, on their passport photos, knew
The sound of a bird being pushed out of its nest.

Because I've become accustomed to failure,
Some smoke of sadness blows off these poems.
These poems are windows blown open by winter wind.

"The Trap-Door"

Often a poet in English will announce the subject of the poem right away "Something there is that doesn't love a wall." Frost then stays on that same subject until the poem is over. That's a fine way to do a poem. But the requirement the classic ghazal makes—and the great gift that form gives—is that the poet is asked to change the subject matter with each stanza. Each stanza should have a new landscape or theme. The abruptness of such changes is probably illustrated best in this particular poem, "The Trap-Door."

One of the old untiring themes of love poetry for centuries has been the fall of lovers from Paradise into ordinary life. This is one of the old Griefs of Mankind, and the idea will be understood by all grown-ups: "Men and women spend only a moment in Paradise." Something excessive is always good when dealing with common sorrow, so I introduced kangaroos, who trundle off with the married couples in their pouch. Some listeners at readings query: "Why kangaroos?" Such a query can't be answered. I say, "Why not?"

The second stanza, mentioning Leghorn, goes to a different theme. Sometimes if I'm reading to city people, I have to remind them that a Leghorn is a chicken. "Why should the Leghorn family praise the knife-grinder?" It seems that God has a lot to do besides loving human beings. We may recall that the Lisbon earthquake, which killed thousands of good-hearted Portuguese Christians in 1756, troubled all of Europe for decades. Blake said, "The wrath of the lion is the wisdom of God."

Writing poems of this sort with their wild assertions and exaggerations is a little like seeing blood on the walls of your room. When I suddenly saw mice running, the stanza became funny without my intending it, and the mice are running off the see Tennyson.

The rest of the poem moves toward an appreciation of Muslim culture and civilization. As we know, Muslim writers and scientists did very advanced work in the Middle Ages. They achieved fantastic work in astronomy at that time; that's why so many stars—such as Aldebaran—have Arabic names. Their scholars also translated many ancient Greek writers such as Plotinus and the Greek alchemists into Arabic. Later in Spain, Western scholars, still not knowing Greek themselves, translated these texts from Arabic into Spanish.

One of the great young men among the Arabs was named Jabir; he studied the alchemical meaning of sound. His genius was such that people could feel holiness radiating out from any one of his sentences. Our revenge on him was to call all that "gibberish."

Medieval culture, both in the Muslim world of the Sufis and in the Christian world of the Troubadours, praised lovers. The attitude always was that even though lovers tend to be skinny and rejected by the parents of the women they loved, some great joy came from them. Many of them were paupers, but they would wake up in the morning "playing the flute of gratitude."

The Trap Door

Men and women spend only a moment in Paradise.
Then a trap-door sends them down to the Lords of Misreason,
Where baby kangaroos carry us all off in their small pouches.

Let's all praise the saints who never mention God!
Why should the Leghorn family praise the Knife-Grinder?
I don't think it's right for water to assist the grindstone, either.

The walls of my poetry house are splashed with blood.
I don't want to be inward. Every day a thousand mice
Run out of my door heading for Tennyson's house.

Arabs with big eyes studied all night for years
And translated the Tablets of the Alchemists.
They could pull Mercury from the knees of the wind.

Jabir the Brilliant at fourteen could arrange
Sounds so they became holy. Friends, each day
I crawl over and kiss some of the books I love.

It is because the lovers have been exiled
To the non-existence of the onion fields
That the pauper wakes up playing the flute of gratitude.

"The Old St. Peter by Rembrandt"

I began this poem at the Art Institute in Chicago, where, a couple of years ago, I saw one of the last of Rembrandt's portraits of St. Peter. Peter, as you recall, was in Jerusalem with the disciples during those days when Jesus was arrested, tried, sentenced and executed. The night following their teacher's death, the Roman CIA was looking for people who might have been a part of that network. A Roman soldier confronted Peter, and Peter said basically, "I just got in town." He felt enormous grief and shame for that act of cowardice. The deeply human fear that led to his "denial" always interested Rembrandt, and Rembrandt returned to Peter again and again. One of his paintings shows three or four men sitting around a small fire, and we see a Roman centurion wearing a steel breastplate. The breastplate reflects the light of a Christian's candle. I mention that scene in this poem. Rembrant's portrait shows St. Peter, about 80 years old, still feeling his cowardice, and his face very worn—one hand is lifted above his head.

Once I had written about the steel breastplate and the candle, the ghazal form required me to change the subject matter. How firmly do our friends hold us in their affections? If Peter could so easily forget his teacher, couldn't our friends as easily forget us? When our friends are not with us, perhaps we begin to drift away, as the parentless child may drift into outer space.

How much sustained devotion and faithfulness do we have? We are probably masters of unfaithfulness; in fact probably the descendants of the unfaithful in Norway or Sweden. What makes us so sure that our grandmothers and grandfathers were people of faith? We don't know.

Since the ghazal form requires me to change the subject matter again, I remembered how it felt in January of the new millennium when we looked back on the 20th century now over. Slavery is now once more a major activity in the Sudan; Europeans and Americans who care are buying back slaves and returning them to their villages. Obviously a massive stealing of slaves in the 18th century led to the work force for the plantations in the South and some of those stony farms in New England. The atomic bomb was invented in the 20th century and used in Japan; over two million people died in the Second World War, dwarfing any wars of the 18th and 19th century. "The whole century has been a defeat." Neruda must have felt something like that in 1935 when he said, "It so happens I'm sick of being a human being."

The last stanza goes back to the Rembrandt painting in Chicago: The sense of defeat that so many of us felt at the end of the 20th century seems to be present in Rembrandt's painting of Peter. A beam of light does come from above the painting, and falls on his face. It is not clear that we are any braver than that old man, and it's too late now to redo the last century.

The Old St. Peter by Rembrandt

Noah's ship does not sail with its elephants forever.
The crying of the monkeys breaks off and starts again.
Even shame does not last a whole lifetime.

"It was dark," Peter said. "We were alone. We had
A single candle which shone on the steel breastplate
Of the Roman soldier. The whole town was asleep."

We are bubbles on the lips of our friends.
Each time they turn their heads, we drift toward the Pole;
We pass into the Many and return.

Who can say, "With God, the rest is nothing"?
Who can say, "I am a grandchild of the unfaithful"?
Who is able to wait one month to drink water?

We fell into weeping yesterday at five o'clock.
We wept because slavery has returned; we wept
Because the whole century has been a defeat.

Oh Peter! Peter! The night behind you is black.
A beam of light falls on your outworn face.
What can you do but lift up your hand for forgiveness?

Chicago Museum of Art

"The Battle of Ypres, 1915"

The First World War still remains a source of utter amazement, and to military historians, a cause of dismay. People on both sides thought it would be over in a few weeks. As it happened, trench warfare made its appearance. Like some huge hostile animal, it sat on the Germans, the French, and the English for so many months that half a generation of young men died. *All Quiet on the Western Front* describes trench warfare; and Hitler, we now know, hated it so much he would not allow its author to remain in Germany. In the trenches around Ypres in 1915, 100,000 men died in one day. Three thousand died in the Twin Towers, and that was a heavy blow, but Europe felt a shock 33 times larger on that day.

The sacrifice of young men—in smaller numbers—were, as we know, a common occurrence in the ancient world. Adonis, Attis, and Tammuz were interchangeable names given over generations to certain young males who, some say, represented spring vegetation. They died in early summer. Apparently these sacrifices went on in northern Europe as well. We recall the sacrificed man found in a peat bog in Denmark, his last sacrificial meal of grain still in his stomach. These sacrifices were considered to be relatively routine at that time.

I saw photos one day of the way snake-catchers in India capture the 30-foot-long snakes. Naked men crawl into tunnels after them; and the snakes allows himself or herself to be pulled out backwards. We could say that consumer society is just as clever in getting young people to leave their place of safety, and join a corporation.

Changing the subject, I mention that the Mayans believe that every bit of iron we pull out of the earth and shape we have to pay for. It is Martín Prechtel, that marvelous teacher, who spent 17 years in Guatemala, much of it as ritual leader in a Mayan village, who has brought that concept to this country. Simply shaping a single knife among the Mayans may require several hours of ritual. Our habit in the West is simply to extract the iron—with not a word of ritual or gratitude—then shape it into tanks or elegant cars. "At Ypres we paid dearly for the Bentley car."

As we all know, something in war feels right to human beings as a race. People feel they have an exciting life at last, when TV shows scenes of the fighting. During the recent war in Serbia, the media was waiting for the bombing to commence; on the day the bombing was canceled, I sensed a disappointment in the media and in many people.

So many things with us go wrong these days, and it seems the more technologically advanced we are, the more things go wrong. Because of elaborate technology, anthrax can be sent in a simple envelope; if a nuclear plant fails, the whole of the Ukraine is poisoned.

The last stanza comes from seeing so many newsreels of the start of World War II. We see men and women dancing in the streets of Paris the day war is declared. They are dancing also in Berlin and Vienna. That gaiety doesn't last long. A second later, it seems, we see newsreels of Belgians hauling away their goods and their children in horse carts. CNN calls the recent coverage "America's New War." People fall again and again into excitement on the morning of war.

The Battle at Ypres, 1915

Tammuz, bright with feathers, goes to the Underworld.
The peat-bog man sleeps on his slanted face.
Not to worry; it means that spring has come.

Naked men crawl into tunnels to retrieve the giant
Snakes. They don't resist if pulled out backwards.
Ah, friends, the world pulls us out backwards.

Some say that every bit of iron we pull
Out of the earth, and shape, we have to pay for.
At Ypres we paid dearly for the Bentley car.

Some greedy part hankers for disaster, for things
To go wrong, for the war to start. Many people
Are disappointed when the bombing is canceled.

Events at times turn out exactly wrong with us.
The Magi are misled by a satellite in the night;
And a rabbit sacrifices people during our Easter.

How happy the Europeans were in 1914!
It seemed as though spring had come at last!
Our gaiety the morning of war is momentary.

For Martín Prechtel

"The Storyteller's Way"

I believe that storytelling is one of the great arts, up there with classical music and Greek sculpture. The greatest storyteller in the country now is Gioia Timpanelli, and this poem was written for her. Storytellers always tell each other how difficult it is to be faithful to the story, not to add something extraneous nor leave out parts that don't please you on any given day. So I decided to choose the word "faithful" as the repeating word. Another requirement of the classic ghazal—an order not obeyed by all ghazal writers—is that the same word should end the last line of every stanza. One could say this word, which might be "dawn" or "soul" or "again," carries a whole world with it. Part of the joy in listening to a ghazal is to see how the writer will manage to bring that chosen word in again and again. I mention in the first stanza that the storyteller's job is to be faithful to the tales of infidelity, as well as the tales of faithfulness. The job of the storyteller is to evoke the unfaithful.

That brings up the question, what is our job—the job of us ordinary human beings? Everyone will give a different answer to that question, and our answers will change as one gets older. One answer is that our task is not to insist on holding on to life or holding on to happiness. We could say that the light-hearted grasshopper's way is the way of the faithful.

I am always amazed at the confident tone with which astrologers talk of the marriage of Venus and Mars, or Mercury going backward this week, or Saturn returning every 28 years, or the various adventures that Pluto has in one's chart. The schools train most of our students to be literalists—"A job is a job," "The main thing in life is to show up," etc. So the metaphorical language of astrology is difficult for us to accept. But perhaps the astrologers are right that the stars are faithful.

The next stanza is my favorite stanza in this poem. The lines come from watching jellyfish move so swiftly around inside aquariums or in the Caribbean Sea. Sometimes thousands of jellyfish will be alive in one acre of water. They all seem to be faithful.

Sometimes in stories, the King and the Queen are the defenders of the faithful; sometimes not. The storyteller needs subtle language and subtlety in voice to convey that mysterious moment when the ego or the King decides to betray the faithful.

When we tell stories of our own life, it's often surprising how clearly we remember the times when we failed to do something, when we didn't go to the funeral, or didn't speak up at the crucial moment. Half the sentences in the second half of our life often begin with, "I still feel bad that I didn't . . ." The times when we get in touch with a friend or go to a funeral could be called "exchanging places with the unfaithful."

The Storyteller's Way

It's because the storytellers have been so faithful
That all these tales of infidelity come to light.
It's the job of the faithful to evoke the unfaithful.

Our task is to eat sand, our task is to be sad,
Our task is to cook ashes, our task is to die.
The grasshopper's way is the way of the faithful.

Even though you are a literalist, accept
The invitation to go to Pluto's wedding.
Haven't you learned yet that the stars are faithful?

For every planet, there are a million jellyfish
Shooting along who don't know night from morning.
So is the sea full of the unfaithful or the faithful?

A storyteller has to remember every turn
Of language so that we all know the moment
When the King decides to betray the faithful.

Every story I tell reveals how many tokens
Of loyalty I have forgotten, how often
I have exchanged places with the unfaithful.

For Gioia Timpanelli

WRITING A POEM WHILE LISTENING TO MUSIC

I suppose a true collaboration of music and poetry would happen when the musician and the poet were both in the room, so that each one's art could mingle with the other's. But one musician I am very fond of, the singer Shahram Nazeri, is in Iran.

So collaboration for me has meant listening to Nazeri's voice as well as to the kamancheh and the drummers who are with him, and then trying, in the very moment that I am hearing, to set down a few words that aim to fly into that high, wordless intensity that the music has reached. We all know that notes can remain in their spiritual heaven a long time—perhaps forever—but our words tend to have mud in their shoes and soon fall back to earth. Words ascend sometimes and then fall down again into their earthy nests. Words are tied to death and mud, to night and day.

Still on a good day some linkages may go on. I'll choose as an example a new poem of mine called "Listening to Shahram Nazeri." Nazeri is a contemporary Iranian singer who, like his compatriot Shadjarian, sings the classic modes. The words they sing, adapted to the mode that pleases them, may come from a poem of Attar or Rumi or Hafez. Some of the airs or tunes they depend on are hundreds of years old. The music in this particular song has relations to Mongolian horse-music; one can hear in it the rhythm of horses' hooves. So the first line comes from that rhythm.

> I know the horses keep galloping for miles.

The notes seem to ascend, and so I said:

> I know the ants keep lifting their feelers to heaven
> And planning new triumphs, but it's already too late!

The ghazal form, as we know, likes to have the same word or phrase placed at the close of each stanza. So even in the first stanza, the closing of each following stanza is already decided. It's too late to change it! The poems that Nazeri is drawing on often pull in powerful images from the old spiritual poets; there are always hints of Adam and the loss of the Garden.

> When Nazeri sings, I don't care if the Second

Adam comes down or not; I don't care if my words
Get you to cry or not—it's already too late.

The mood of the music often reminds the listener of desert camps and the keening of women at gravesites.

The smell of coffee spreads out from the fire.
The wild-haired old women sing over the coffin.
Go on complaining and crying. It's already too late!

The powerful singing and the drumbeat of the timbres seem to pull images directly out of the listener's word-store. The syllables and the drumbeats seem to belong to those of us who are listening.

I know sweet vowels and inescapable rhythms.
I know how sweet it is when a young woman is here
And the old men think of God; but it's already too late.

Words and images appear in our heads that would never appear if we were sitting in some silent room. The abundance of grief that is called into the music and nourished there reminds us how far grief is from complaint and disappointment.

My tongue never becomes bitter because my mouth
Keeps holding the grief-pipe between my teeth.
Go on and conquer bitterness; it's already too late.

The intensity of Iranian classical music and the triumphant beauty of Shahram Nazeri's voice are able to return us to some early morning of our own lives.

Here I am; I am all alone. It's early morning.
I am so happy. How can so much grandeur
Live beneath my skin? Go on asking; it's already too late!

My poem is a poor, flawed attempt to collaborate with the music. I'm interested too in collaboration with painting. We could write for another thousand years while listening to music—there is no need to hurry—it's already too late!

Listening to Shahram Nazeri

I know the horses keep galloping for miles.
I know the ants keep lifting their feelers to heaven
And planning new triumphs, but it's already too late!

When Nazeri sings, I don't care if the Second
Adam comes down or not; I don't care if my words
Get you to cry or not—it's already too late.

The smell of coffee spreads out from the fire.
The wild-haired old women sing over the coffin.
Go on complaining and praying. It's already too late!

I know sweet vowels and inescapable rhythms.
I know how sweet it is when a young woman is here
And the old men think of God; but it's already too late.

My tongue never becomes bitter because my mouth
Keeps holding the grief pipe between my teeth.
Go on and conquer bitterness; it's already too late.

Here I am; I am all alone. It's early morning.
I am so happy. How can so much grandeur
Live beneath my skin? Go on asking; it's already too late!

IV.

NO ONE WRITES ALONE

THE *PARIS REVIEW* INTERVIEW

I. Time at Harvard

Interviewer: Could you talk about your earliest connections to poetry?

Robert Bly: A beautiful high school teacher interested me in poetry. I think I wrote a poem for her saying that Tojo was a bad person. In the Navy I met the first person I'd known who actually wrote poetry, a man named Eisy Eisenstein. We conspired to flunk out of the radar program on the grounds that we were poets who couldn't be bothered with science. We didn't succeed. Once out of the Navy, I entered St. Olaf College, which is an old Norwegian Lutheran hangout—a Bly was a dean there. My freshman English teacher, to my amazement, excused me from freshman English when I turned in my first piece. That was a generous move; I joined an upperclassmen creative writing group. A woman my age wrote poetry; I fell in love with her, and I wrote a poem to her. I had the strangest sensation. I felt something in the poem I hadn't intended to put there. It was as if "someone else was with me."

Interviewer: Could we talk a little about your beginning poems at Harvard?

Bly: I came to Harvard in the fall of 1947, after having been in the Navy for two years. Robert Creeley, who was there the year before, remarked later that there is something heroic in every writer of our generation, perhaps from the awareness that we had won the war. He mentions somewhere that the standards of American literature were very high at the time—Eudora Welty, Hemingway, Eliot, Stevens, Cummings, Charles Olson. He felt it was our job to keep those standards up.

Interviewer: He also said that your generation felt it was their job to put the culture back together again. Everything was in tatters.

Bly: Yes, there was that mood. The *Harvard Advocate* had just started up again with its memories and mementos of Eliot and Stevens, who had written for it. Bob Crichton and Bill Emerson took me in, and I took in Don Hall, and we both took in John Ashbery, against much pressure from the trustees of the *Advocate,* I might add. The night Bill Emerson and Bob Crichton interviewed me for the board, I answered one of their questions with a critical overview of American poetry since 1910. When I finished, one of them said, "It was good of you to tell us these things." But they took me. We published Adrienne Rich, who was at Radcliffe, and that early poem of John Ashbery's "Some Trees." We stayed up late at night arguing over the next issue. By the way, Adrienne was not allowed to enter the Poetry Room at the new Lamont Library, because the founders said it was for men! That's wild! No one seriously questioned that.

An amazing group of writers were at Harvard at that time. Because of the war, the classes of 1949, 1948 and 1947 were bunched up along with the class of 1950. Archibald MacLeish had been hired away from being Director of the Library of Congress. The young writers gathered around him and Albert Guerard, a fine teacher of essay and fiction writing, an American version of a European intellectual. The group I remember included John Hawkes, Bob Crichton, Kenneth Koch, Donald Hall, Frank O'Hara, L. E. Sissman, John Ashbery, a fine fiction writer named Milton Hughes, whom I've never heard of again, Adrienne Rich, George Plimpton, and many others. Richard Wilbur, a bit older, was in town, and Robert Frost stayed in Boston during the spring and fall.

Archibald MacLeish had a little trouble with us. He was a generous man, but was not prepared to be in the midst of a group of veterans. We were a little older than the normal students, and even though many, like myself, had never been in combat, we were still not about to take orders from someone simply because he was well-known. In class MacLeish might remark, "My friend, Ezra Pound, wrote this poem:

> See, they return; ah, see the tentative
> Movements, and the slow feet,
> The trouble in the pace and the uncertain
> Wavering!"

Someone would say, "That's awful. It's crap. Do you have any friends who are better poets?" And so on. We liked him, but we held his feet to the fire. The classes, unlike the scenes at the Library of Congress, were confrontational.

Interviewer: Were you one of the irascible ones?

Bly: Oh, of course. I puffed up my throat like an iguana. MacLeish felt too calm to us, not intense enough. I wasn't the worst one, but I was one of them. One day after three classes or so, he called me into the office and said, "Robert, you know, this thing can't continue in the way it's going. Either you change your behavior in class, or I'll have to jump out the window." And I said, "Well, jump." I was young; I wanted to show off. He had similar conversations with others, and the upshot was that he didn't meet the class anymore that year; we saw him only one by one. I think he didn't meet any classes for the next three years, until the veterans had all graduated. But it heartened us that MacLeish knew Hemingway and even Pound. We felt we had some contact with writers who really mattered. We weren't touching them, of course, but we weren't that far away either.

Interviewer: You became the literary editor of the *Advocate*?

Bly: I did. We had a lot to choose from, and we learned a lot arguing over poems and stories. We published our own work as well. I recall reviewing a new book of poems by William Carlos Williams.

Interviewer: Wasn't that a little unusual? He was much out of fashion then. Certainly your teachers didn't mention him; they were in Robert Penn Warren and Eliot's camp, or MacLeish's.

Bly: I guess that's true. Williams did feel ignored and hated. I suppose I found his poems in the Grolier Book Shop. Gordon Cairnie ran it. Eliot had met Conrad Aiken in that bookstore; there was a sort of poets' sofa. Poets sat on it. Gordon might say to some freshman who had just wandered in, "Would you take care of the shop for ten minutes?" Then he might not come back for twenty-four hours! To the poets, that store was a home.

William Carlos Williams was the one who meant the most to me, so I hitchhiked to see him, from Cambridge to Paterson, wearing my chino pants, and I called him from a bar nearby. "Could I come to see you?" "Sure, come on, kid." So he let me in, and said, "Sit down over there. Do you write poetry?" "Well, yeah, I guess so. . .I suppose." He went about his business, planning his deliveries, and typing something. He glanced at me from time to time. After fifteen minutes or so, he said, "Okay, kid, you can go now." He understood that I just wanted to *look* at him. I drifted out, floating along the street. It was heavenly.

But we also admired Eliot, and felt close to him because he'd published his earliest poems in the *Advocate*. When the *Advocate* nearly went broke in my senior year, I suggested we put out a surefire issue, reprinting Eliot's poems. The excuse was that the issue was "In Honor of His Sixtieth Birthday." But I proofread the cover badly, and it said, "Sixteenth Birthday." That was bizarre. A couple of weeks later I got a letter from him that said something like:

> Dear Mr. Bly,
>
> I was very surprised upon opening a copy of the *Harvard Advocate* recently to find my early poems published there. If I had wanted to reprint these poems, I should have done so myself.
>
> Yours sincerely
>
> T. S. Eliot

Well, it was disgraceful. But even receiving a scolding letter from T. S. Eliot made us feel a part of a community of serious writers. When Don Hall went to Oxford a year or so later, he took the opportunity to apologize to Eliot, and had a good conversation with him in his long, skinny office!

2. Time in New York

Interviewer: Did you go to Oxford or some such place as well?

Bly: No. I think I had spent up my available capital for extroversion in college, and I had to be by myself. I intended to take one year, but ended up taking four. At the start I lived in a small cabin in northern Minnesota through fall and winter. I lived by shooting partridge illegally; I wanted to write like Milton. The next year, the summer of 1951, I moved to New York, where I lived for three more years, excessively alone. "Altarwise by owl light in the halfway house," as Dylan Thomas put it.

I lived in tiny rooms—the better ones had a hot plate—and was determined to write twelve hours a day at least six days a week. And did. To support myself I worked one day a week, as a file clerk or a typist and for a while, a painter, carrying around my painter's bag with the coveralls. When one is living what the French call the garret life, it's surprising how often one meets someone with the odd instinct to help. I'd go to a certain employment agency for painting jobs, and would usually get fired by noon. Jack, at the agency, was never upset. He'd send me back out. "Getting fired is nothing." He guessed I wanted solitude. Finally he assigned me as the only painter of the inside of a huge warehouse in Brooklyn. Every Thursday I'd get one patch of some enormous wall painted blue, and then I'd come back next Thursday and so on. I don't know what he told the owners. "Why isn't that job done?" "I don't know, some of the guys have been sick. It's hard to get good help." A doctor even tried to help me during a VA checkup for a heart murmur I'd taken on after rheumatic fever in the Navy. As a disability, it provided a small check. He said, "Well, I don't hear a thing. But the murmur might come back, and I'll say you still have one so your check will keep coming. You look as if you need one."

***Interviewer*:** Did you try to make money through your writing?

***Bly*:** The only money I earned by writing during those years was from two poems printed in the very first issue of *The Paris Review*. The other day I found a letter to my mother from that time that shows I kept close track of how many copies sold in New York.

***Interviewer*:** Did you try fiction?

***Bly*:** I wanted to be a playwright, and wrote a play called *Martin Luther*. The trouble was that no one in my family talked. Eugene O'Neill's family suffered, but they talked. That effort was hopeless from the start.

If you work only one day a week, you can't afford a good room. At one point I sublet a studio in a building on the east side of Washington Square from a woman who taught art at Brooklyn College; she used the studio on the weekends. She rented her studio to me for day use, not realizing I slept there and had no other home. I had to evade the guards at night when I went to the bathroom, which was on the floor below, and I slept Saturday nights in Grand Central Station. I spent most of my days writing ten-line iambic poems.

Interviewer: Were they nature poems, of the sort Richard Wilbur, whom you admired, wrote?

Bly: No. And I didn't want to write private poems. Because of Yeats, I wanted to bring history in. So I would choose some incident from Greek or Roman history, say, the murder of Archimedes by an inattentive soldier, and try to make it stand for something much bigger. My work couldn't be accused of being timely. I also worked on translating Pindar, another hopeless cause.

Interviewer: Did you meet any other poets during this time?

Bly: New York was lonely then. Poets were reading only at the Y. I had one or two friends from college, but met no new poets. For a while I lived in a room I rented from an old portrait painter from the South on West 67th Street. He painted faithfully there everyday and was disappointed because they wouldn't hang his paintings anymore in the front room of the Salmagundi Club. He was 65 or 70 years old; I was 26. And together we'd walk five or six blocks west and buy three-day-old bread from the bakery and then walk home again. We were on both sides of success—too young and too old.

Interviewer: How long did you live this way?

Bly: In New York?

Interviewer: Yes.

Bly: Three years. I can't tell you how odd it was. I sometimes didn't talk for a month. I was a homemade monk, but with no one to serve me food. No, I wasn't a monk. I was stuck.

The solitude was a big pause after years of activity. But I lost something too. The poems I wrote at Harvard were not great, but they enjoyed some language that we inhabit together surreptitiously; people could hear what I was saying. Last month I read some of the journals I kept during those three years. I grew alarmed because I could see myself losing the common language that we, as humans, have. Word after word had disappeared into some huge hole. Later, a dear friend, a Korean writer, Kim Yong Ik, said,

"You use 'tears' several times in this poem, but you don't mean by that word what the rest of us mean, so the poem doesn't work." He was right. I have spent many years since trying to recover a common language, one that can cross the distance between people.

So those solitary years had a dark side. Yet there was something deliberate in it. After all, why shouldn't we lose that common language with which we often say so little? Sometimes it offers only social chatter. Balzac in *Louis Lambert* mentions certain ideas that are "antagonistic to the social stream." When his character meets Louis Lambert, he feels "a desire to plunge into the infinite." So those three years of solitude didn't offer much living, but it was an experience of the vertical, contrasted to the horizontal mode of everyday social life.

Interviewer: How did this time in New York end?

Bly: It ended when MacLeish, whom I visited in Cambridge, sent me on a wild-goose chase to Iowa to pick up some money the Rockefeller Foundation had put up for writers. He noticed that I was a little gaunt, and he said, "I'll put you up for this grant. Just find another older writer to recommend you and it's done." I bought a car for $65 and drove west, stopping in Bloomington to hear John Crowe Ransom lecture. He was fantastic. I sent him some poems, and he said something like:

> Dear Mr. Bly:
>
> Thank you for sending these poems to me. Some of them I like very much. I think you could publish them almost anywhere. Many of them are fine.
>
> Yours sincerely,
> John Crowe Ransom

It's remarkable that he would write to me at all.

Meanwhile, the other writer had forgotten to send his recommendation; and so, when I got to Iowa City, the grant was gone. I remember driving into Iowa City for the first time, seeing those low, nondescript buildings, and saying, "What kind of country is this when a great poet like Robert Lowell has to teach in a place that looks like this?" I must have expected buildings like the British Parliament houses, or the Louvre.

I asked for a job teaching, and they said if I joined the Writer's Workshop I could have a job, though I had no qualifications. I taught one course of Freshman English and one called "Greeks and the Bible." Teaching was a sudden immersion in the hot water of sociability! I was so afraid, it took me two weeks to be able to stand up behind my desk. I loved teaching, but got too involved in the students' lives. I wrote very few poems that year. I was able to recover enough received language to teach, but the language for poetry was still gone.

Interviewer: Wasn't John Berryman teaching there that year?

Bly: Yes, he was. There was always a little drinking trouble around him. I was buying toothpaste one morning, and the drugstore radio said that the police had picked up John trying to break into his own apartment the night before. This was a wholesome state university. I said, "There goes John." He remarked that there was only one man in the country who would understand what had happened without asking a single question; he called Allen Tate in Minneapolis. Allen said, "Come to Minneapolis, John." So John taught for years in the Humanities Department at the University of Minnesota and was marvelous. Philip Levine wrote an essay called "Mine Own John Berryman" in his book *The Bread of Time*, about Berryman's teaching at Iowa, making clear the high voltage of his seminars. It's the best essay ever written on a teacher-poet.

Interviewer: How long were you at Iowa?

Bly: I was there a year. In 1955 I married Carol Bly, whom I had known at Harvard and in New York. We moved to an old farm my father had saved for me. We stayed there 25 years. It was a half-mile from the one I grew up on. I still hadn't shed my isolation; the nearness to my parents was difficult, as was the lack of work. I spent whole days sitting out in the fields. But there was peace. I still had a great love of silence. I collected the poems I wrote there in *Silence in the Snowy Fields*, which came out in 1962. I like that book, and I never would have written a book that interesting if I had not moved back to the country where I was a child.

3. Snowy Fields

Interviewer: What was the mood of poetry in the late Fifties?

Bly: I started a poem the other day that goes this way:

> There was a moment in '58
> In which we thought—
> And we were right—that poetry
> Our poetry—would bless everyone.

It's hard to explain. Something fresh could be felt all over the country. Don't believe what you read that the Fifties was a dull time; it wasn't, certainly not in literature. Robert Creeley was publishing the poems later collected in *For Love,* amazing things! Theodore Roethke was laying out his high-spirited poems, and Gary Snyder was publishing the poems later collected in *Rip Rap*. Robert Payne had brought out his great anthology, *The White Pony*. Li Po said:

> If you ask me why I dwell among green mountains,
> I should laugh silently; my soul is serene.
> The peach blossom follows the moving water.
> There is another heaven and earth beyond the world of men.

Hong's book of Tu Fu poems was out—that beautiful green book I still have with me. Some kind of longing was in the air. James Wright felt it:

> Suddenly I realize
> That if I stepped out of my body, I would break
> Into blossom.

The Chinese poems and James Wright's lines are linguistic expressions of the longing that there be "another heaven and earth beyond the world of men." All over the country young poets went expectantly to the mailbox, to find some wild thing like *Kayak* or some little essay by a Buddhist meditator. There wasn't a flood of mail—just one or two delicious pieces, or nothing.

I don't know why that mood of longing appeared in the late Fifties. Perhaps it came because we had won the war. Thousands and thousands of men my age had died. There was a lot of gratitude for that enormous sacrifice. Awe and gratitude were in the air. Maybe we felt—as Creeley suggested—that despite the disintegration, it would be possible for us to put culture back together again. During the war, for example, *Poetry* had about six subscribers. Everything was starting over again.

Or perhaps that wasn't it at all. Maybe the simple delight people felt in air, wind and poems when there was no war was normal. Perhaps everyone felt that way before television held people indoors and fed them bad psychic food. For a few years, we felt, like Yeats in his poem, that

> For twenty minutes, more or less,
> It seemed so great my happiness
> That I was blessed and could bless.

In 1956, I had received a Fulbright Fellowship to do the job of translating some old and new Norwegian poetry into English. Writers my age were aware of good poetry in English, but not the powerful poetry of Chile, Peru, Sweden, Germany, Italy. In the Oslo library I found Pablo Neruda. The moment is still clear to me. The lines were,

> girls sleeping with hands over their hearts,
> dreaming of pirates.

It has an exaggeration there that's so beautiful. It's alive in the heart and flamboyant—so different from T. S. Eliot. I had spent three years at Harvard without ever hearing the name Neruda. One problem with the New Critics—whom I otherwise admire greatly—is that they were blind to material outside the English language.

A new kind of image had appeared, which was the engine, or the angel or the body of a wholly fresh poetry. Cesar Vallejo said,

> I will die in Paris, on a rainy day . . .
> It will be a Thursday, because today, Thursday, setting down
> these lines, I have put my upper armbones on
> wrong . . .

He didn't say, "I have put my suit on wrong." No, "I have put my upper armbones on wrong"!

> And never so much as today have I found myself
> With all the road ahead of me, alone.

And there was Neruda's great poem on death:

> There are cemeteries that are lonely,
> graves full of bones that do not make a sound . . .
> And there are corpses,
> feet made of cold and sticky clay,
> death is inside the bones
> like a barking where there are no dogs. . . .

Astounding! "A barking where there are no dogs."

I had a relatively good literary education, and I felt astonished by these poems, so I thought that other poets my age would be moved also. In 1958, when I got back, Bill Duffy and I started a magazine called *The Fifties.* On the inside front cover, we announced that "most of the poetry published in America today is too old-fashioned." We developed various ways to infuriate people who had submitted old-fashioned poems. One was a card that read:

> This entitles you to buy the new book of Alfred, Lord Tennyson,
> as soon as it is published.

In each issue we awarded the Order of the Blue Toad to an obnoxious literary personage of the day; and we made up a "Madame Tussaud's Wax Museum." In it were lines of John Crowe Ransom or Allen Ginsberg and Longfellow and so on. The whole thing was a little adolescent, but it had some spirit.

Each copy of the beginning issue cost us a dollar, and we sold it for fifty cents, so we weren't doing so well on money. But we sent a copy to everyone who had been included in *New Poets of England and America,* relatively traditional poets—I was one—edited by Donald Hall, Louis Simpson, and Robert Pack. We also listed on the back cover the Europeans we intended to translate and publish.

***Interviewer*:** What responses did you get from the "establishment"?

***Bly*:** One man wrote me, saying, "You know who you are? You're nothing but a Captain Bly pissing up a drainpipe!" That was a strange metaphor. Allen Tate said something like: "So people can write poems that are not in iambic? A cat can walk on its front legs too. So what?" That was another strange metaphor.

James Wright, then at the University of Minnesota, also got a copy of that issue. He noticed Georg Trakl listed among the Europeans to be translated, and he replied with a long letter describing his despair at attempting to interest English Department members in Georg Trakl, whose work he happened upon during a Fulbright to Austria. He came out to the farm for a visit the next week; we embarked then on a translation of Trakl and on a close friendship that continued for twenty-two years until he died in 1980. If I had gotten only one gift from the whole labor of the magazine, that would have been enough.

***Interviewer*:** How did you get submissions for *The Fifties*?

***Bly*:** We put a tiny ad in *Poetry Magazine*, for $25 or so, and received poems of Gary Snyder and David Ignatow immediately, which we printed. We found ourselves to be as well part of the small community of writers outside the United States. One day we got a letter from Boris Pasternak written in purple ink. He thanked us for mentioning him among the poets we wished to translate, praised my translations of Gottfried Benn, and then said something like: "But I must tell you, don't save any space for me. Don't bother yourself with that. I have deviated from my former path and become out of date. Yours sincerely, Boris Pasternak."

***Interviewer*:** What did he mean by "deviated from my former path"?

***Bly*:** He intuited, and rightly so, that we were interested in the same sort of poetry he was devoted to when he was our age, namely the allusive, elegant, inward poetry associated with the French symbolists, whose language longed to intermingle with the spiritual. He and Anna Akhmatova and Marina Tsvetaeva wanted to join Russian poetry to that international stream. However, the suffering of Russia pulled him later to issues more particular to Russia, as one can see in *Dr. Zhivago*. That was a more nationalistic, prosaic world. He thought his poems would no longer be interesting to us. Very humbly, he was warning us of that turn.

Interviewer: Who else was on the staff?

Bly: Well, Carol Bly always took a strong part in the magazine, and made up ads saying, "Strontium 90 Builds Bones." We were all figuring out various ways to try to bother the political and nuclear establishment. James Wright did much editing. We published *The Lion's Tail and Eyes* in 1962, with ten poems each of Bill Duffy's and Jim Wright's and mine, and the year before we published *Twenty Poems of Georg Trakl*.

We had a lot of fun editing. Sometimes Bill and I would get a bottle of Jim Beam, go up north to a cabin and send back all the poems we'd received in one night. He was a genius at rejection slips. "Dear Mr. Smith: These poems remind me of false teeth. Yours sincerely, William Duffy." Or, "These poems are like ice cream that has melted when the refrigerator got turned off." "These poems are like three-day-old lettuce." Then they would write insulting letters back and we'd print the letters.

We published many wonderful poems of Paul Celan and Juan Ramón Jiménez. After a few years, we were ready with *Twenty Poems of Pablo Neruda*, which James and I had translated, and I wrote to him for permission to print the Spanish and the translations. We had paid the Trakl estate $75. I said to Carol, "What do you think? Neruda's so great, let's offer him $150." She said, "Good idea." So I mentioned to him that we didn't have much money, but we could promise that many of the young poets in the U.S. would read the book. He wrote back something like: "I know your Press very well. You were the first ones who printed my brother, César Vallejo. Certainly you may publish my poems. I only have one request: that you send the $150 directly to a certain bookseller in Barcelona. I owe him a lot of money. Yours, Pablo Neruda."

Interviewer: That's a good story. The poems collected in *Snowy Fields*. . . how did they come about?

Bly: I often walked out somewhere and sat down. Usually a poem didn't begin until something happened:

> I rise and walk out in the summery night.
> A dark thing hopped near me in the grass.

The poems didn't move according to something I wanted to say. Usually the second stanza didn't begin until something else had happened. Maybe a leaf fell, or the sunset darkened the tree.

The gratitude we've spoken of was present at the start of the sixties and at Woodstock. People began to feel that there was something that could satisfy the longing, maybe music or drugs. But it's the nature of longing that it cannot be satisfied. That, however, is when that got attached to pop culture.

Interviewer: I remember Joe Langland saying about *Silence in the Snowy Fields* that he felt that both you and Jim Wright had done for American poetry what the Impressionists did for painting, which was to bring the poet outside and allow her or him to record what was going on exactly at the moment the person was out there — so that the poems say: "This is going on right in front of me right now." And in that sense, it felt as if some sort of canvas were outside and you were painting exactly what was happening.

Bly: Well, that's a very great compliment that Joe Langland said. I don't know if we lived up to that. We did what we could. When I wrote poems in those years, I was not someone like Neruda, trying to feel my way back through centuries of human suffering and human grief. I'm sitting beneath a tree and realizing that I'm happy doing that:

> I'm happy in this ancient place,
> A spot easily caught sight of above the corn,
> If I were a young animal ready to turn home at dusk.

That sense of gratitude and longing only lasted four or five years. I don't feel much gratitude in the country now.

Occasionally during those years we'd go to New York and stay a couple of months in the Village, on West 11th Street. I remember a funny afternoon from that time. Don Hall had come back from England to conduct the *Paris Review* interview with T. S. Eliot. Louis Simpson and I wanted him to take us along to the interview. He wouldn't agree. "Come on, Don, we'll die! This is our only chance to meet him!" "No. Robert won't behave himself." So that was that. But on the morning of the interview, Don came over and said, "The tape recorder hasn't worked out. Could I borrow yours?" "Aha!" So we had him. Louis and I went up to Mrs. Cohn's apartment, where Eliot and his wife were staying. She asked us inside to wait a bit, and I realized that in a few minutes T. S. Eliot would walk through the door. What an incredible thing. He did! Don greeted him, and we were introduced, without names, as two tape-recorder technicians. Eliot was kind to us. "Would you like scotch or bourbon?" "Bourbon." "With ice or without?" "With." "I never have ice with bourbon myself." Don then put the recorder down. Eliot sat on the sofa, his wife was off to the right nearby. He threw warm glances toward her whenever a joke came up. So Don and Eliot went through their interview. Eliot answered questions he had avoided, such as, "Is *The Waste Land* a Christian poem?" "Not at all." He said that no American poet had ever interviewed him before. Louis and I stayed over at the far end of the room near the ice, getting drunk on the bourbon. When the interview was over, I went up to Eliot, and said, "You are a wonderful man!" I remember handing him his hat—I think he was going out. I resisted putting it on his head. I knew he would say, "If I had wanted the hat on, I would have put it on myself." But it was a grand day.

4. Translation

Interviewer: May I ask you about translation? You've done a lot. Why?

Bly: Take Tomas Tranströmer. Translation of him was an amazing experience for me because there was a kind of image appearing in him that I'd never seen before. And it's interesting that the Europeans recognized this, and within a few years he was being honored all over Europe. So how can you describe the strange images that he produces?

> We got ready, and showed our house.
> The visitors said, "You live well.
> The slum must be inside you."

One time he was taken into the Swedish army to do his duty for a few weeks. "Sentry Duty":

> Task: to be where I am.
> Even when I'm in this solemn and absurd
> role, I am still the place
> where creation does some work on itself.

This is a far, far reach from French surrealism, whose images don't have a center. They're like a wheel without any spokes.

Interviewer: Can you give us some idea about what that center might be?

Bly:

> Dawn comes. The sparse tree trunks
> take on color now, the frostbitten
> forest flowers form a silent search party
> after something that has disappeared in the dark.

He's so unbelievably fast! He's like some runner, you know, he enters the forest and suddenly he's way gone, he's ahead of you, I don't know where he is. "Forest flowers form a silent search party / after something that has disappeared in the dark." And it's not a teasing thing, exactly, but there's a feeling that Tranströmer is closer to some silent energy in the middle of the universe than the rest of us are. "Things not yet happened are already here! / I feel that. They're just out there. // A murmuring mass outside the barrier. / They can only slip in one by one." That's incredible. "They want to slip in. Why? They do, / one by one. I am the turnstile." That's an amazing thing; he is saying that he is the center of these objects and creatures and images that want to come into the world. But he doesn't say he is a very important center. He's only the turnstile. And that's so beautiful and it's so different from Michelangelo, who says, "I made all this. I am God."

I think I've made my point here, that by trying to translate something like that, the poems come deep inside you, the images come deep inside you, and you no longer say, "Well, Tranströmer is a wonderful poet," or "This is very fresh." You don't say that. You feel yourself, because of the work you've done on the image, invaded by the image. You feel that it has become a part of your house like someone who's moved into your house, and your house is changed then. Your house has changed because these images have come in. So that's the way I feel about translation. It's a blessing.

5. Vietnam Poems

Interviewer: You wrote your first poem against the Vietnam War in 1965. It seems strange that these poems come so soon after the *Snowy Fields* poems in 1962.

Bly: It felt that way to me too. Suddenly everything changed. It was a hard time. No one knew what to do. Some of the older poets—Berryman was one—thought it was bad taste for a poet to participate in a public meeting. (I didn't think so.) At the start none of us had written any protest poems ourselves, so we recited e. e. cummings, William Stafford, I. F. Stone, Robinson Jeffers, et cetera. The Swedish poet Goran Sonnevi wrote the first good poem about the war, and we read that poem in English. After a few months, a number of poets of all stripes joined an umbrella organization David Ray and I set up called American Writers Against the Vietnam War. The first read-in we did was at Reed College—I think Ferlinghetti was there. Louis Simpson helped a lot. The veterans of World War II, like Louis, whose company was wiped out at Bastogne, were effective when right-wingers shouted at us from the balcony, "You're all cowards!" "Go back to Russia!"

Galway Kinnell and I sometimes joined to do a series of readings. Once in upstate New York we gave three readings in one day, flying from Albany to Syracuse to Buffalo. That night we ended up at a diner. Suddenly a drunk in the diner, not knowing anything about us at all, said, "You want to know what I did during the Korean War?" "Well, what did you do?" "I was a rear gunner. We were coming back from a bombing raid, and the pilot for some reason flew right down the main street of this little Korean town. I had some ammunition left. You know what I did? I lowered my guns and shot every Korean I could see walking on either side of the street. What do you think about that? Why did I do that?" That's what that time was like. Old stuff came up.

Most of the English teachers in the universities hated our doing "political poems," as they were called. That still happens. When I'm at a reception at a university these days, an English professor may come up to me and ask: "How do you feel now about those poems you wrote during the war?" They want me to disown the poems. I say, "I'm sorry I didn't write more of them."

Interviewer: Were you thinking of Whitman when you wrote "The Teeth Mother Naked at Last?"

Bly: Well, the long Whitman line seemed proper. "Wings appear over the trees, wings with eight hundred rivets."

Robert Duncan wrote the lines:

                                        the hell of
America's unacknowledged, unrepented crimes that I saw in
        Goldwater's eyes
now shines from the eyes of the President
        in the swollen head of the nation.

So Whitman's work was the model. The longer lines require to be lifted, as Whitman's are, by an increasing or persisting energy. Long lines are flung out. It was as if they were held up by the same sort of energy that holds up the plane's wings—the same sort of energy that supported the protestors during that long war.

Actually, I had been working on political poetry for several years before the war started. I was looking at American history from the point of view of Jacob Boehme, who insisted on distinguishing the outward man from the inward man. These poems were printed in a book called *The Light Around the Body*, along with some of the poems about Vietnam.

Interviewer: That book received the National Book Award in 1968, which resulted in the famous speech you gave at the National Book Awards night.

Bly: That speech did cause some controversy. I said that there is something wrong in complimenting ourselves on our literary grandness when we are destroying a culture that probably has a longer literary tradition than we have.

Interviewer: You gave the $1,000 check to a Resistance member, as I recall, during the speech.

Bly: I went down to the Resistance office in lower Manhattan, and said, "I know how you guys can get a thousand dollars." They said, "That's great! How do we do it?" "Just have someone come to the Book Awards ceremony tomorrow night, and I'll pass the check to him." They said, "It should be someone with a suit. I know someone who has a suit!" That was charming.

Interviewer: If the Vietnam War happened again, or now, would you spend all that energy and time protesting it?

Bly: Certainly.

6. Sound in Poetry

Interviewer: Can I ask you something about the element of sound, what it means in poems? You've been giving talks on that lately.

Bly: Wallace Stevens says something like, "A poem should almost successfully escape the intellect." Only music can do that. So that if the poem has no genius in sound, the practical intellect will imprison it, so to speak, in a box and show it to visitors.

Interviewer: You are thinking of a poem as a musical event, as well as a carrier of thoughts or emotions?

Bly: Exactly. Poems can become musical events in a number of ways. Two I've been brooding on are these. First, the Seven Holy Vowels, as they were understood in ancient times, can come in. (Josceyln Godwin has a charming book called *The Mystery of the Seven Vowels*.) The great vowels bring radiance and add energy when they enter; they even encourage the arms and legs to move in a certain way. The seven vowels, one could say, penetrate through the intellect to the body. Then there is such a thing as chiming. *Chiming* means that tiny sounds chime with each other inside the line. It's a sort of interior rhyming that the writer does without alerting, or even telling, the reader.

Suppose you decide like Stevens to chime with the syllable *in*. Then you could say:

> The trade wind jingles the rings in the nets around the rocks
>   by the docks on Indian River.

It is the choice of *in* that determines the name of the river at the end. One little chiming poem of mine begins:

> How sweet to weight the line with all these vowels:
> Body, Thomas, the codfish's psalm. The gaiety
> Of form lies in the labor of its playfulness.

Later it goes:

> The chosen sound reappears like the evening star
> In the solemn return the astronomers love.

Most good poems have repeating sounds. But one can make chiming into a sort of principle. If the chiming sound returns three times, it becomes a tune. Then the whole stanza turns to music.

7. Camphor and Gopherwood

***Interviewer*:** When the war was over, were you finally able to spend more time with your writing, with your wife and your children? What did you write then?

***Bly*:** I tried to do a long initiatory or autobiographical poem called "Sleepers Joining Hands." I worked on it a long time, but it never really cohered, probably because I didn't have enough solitude during those years. The protests took a lot of time, and I needed to earn money as well for the children, who were going to college eventually.

***Interviewer*:** Wasn't that the time you also began the prose poems collected in *This Body Is Made of Camphor and Gopherwood*?

Bly: Oh, those were better! Those were sweet! I owe those to Kabir and Rumi. *Camphor and Gopherwood* were my first "Beloved" poems. I wrote them while sitting on the floor of my meditation corner, struggling with Tagore's English for Kabir and Arbery's English for Rumi. For about four years there was the absolute delight of writing these *Camphor and Gopherwood* poems, and writing also a number of poems in lines which were gathered in a book called *Loving a Woman in Two Worlds.*

Ruth Counsell entered my life in 1972. Carol Bly and I agreed to divorce in 1979, and Ruth Counsell and I were married the next year.

Interviewer: It seems odd to me that these love poems—so passionate—should come relatively late in your life—you must have been 46 or so in 1972. Why weren't they written in your twenties?

Bly: There's something backward about my life . . . so many things happen out of time. I suppose I spent—or wasted—much of my twenties alone in a New York room, during the years I've described. At that time I couldn't be both a lover and an artist, so I decided to be an artist only. But these late-arriving things cause a lot of suffering and grief for others.

Interviewer: How was *Loving a Woman in Two Worlds* received?

Bly: With alert indifference. Fred Chappell reviewed the book in *The New York Times Book Review* and said it wasn't a real book of love poems because there wasn't enough hatred and anger in it. In a way, he's right, but only in a thoroughly modern way. That book has links to the 13th century French and German troubadours. It's about seven centuries out of date.

Interviewer: Why are so few love poems written today?

Bly: A lot of angry love poems are written. Is that an answer?

Interviewer: Not to me.

Bly: Yeats broods about that in his poem "The Two Trees." He says one tree, a holy tree, grows in the heart. The other tree is full of the "ravens of unresting thought." It's hard to get out of the raven tree, whether you are a man or a woman. It was Kabir and Rumi who helped me get away from the "ravens of unresting thought." One of the poems in *Loving a Woman in Two Worlds* goes this way:

> Every breath taken in by the man
> Who loves, and the woman who loves,
> Goes to fill the water tank
> Where the spirit horses drink.

8. Men's Work

***Interviewer*:** Your life has been so entirely occupied with writing poetry, editing and translating poems, how did your work with men come about?

***Bly*:** It happened through my teaching. On the farm I was never able to support myself by writing, even though I translated a book from the Danish called *Reptiles and Amphibians of the World,* followed by a translation of Knut Hamsun's *Hunger* from the Norwegian. After that I did *The Story of Gösta Berling,* translated from the Swedish of Selma Lagerlöf. I also did some short stories of Strindberg, which didn't get published. I loved translating fiction but, as it turned out, I couldn't support a family on that.

During the seventies I had a longing to learn something about mythology, and so I printed up a poster announcing a conference on the Great Mother. That was in 1975. About 45 people came to a woods camp in Colorado. It was there I told my very first fairy tale. It was a Celtic story with castles and old ladies and some toads and so on. The implications of it for the growth of an adult person were astounding. I told the story poorly, but we discussed it well. I wasn't the first to have discovered that many of the classic fairy tales lay out stages of initiation into adulthood, which we've entirely forgotten, that our ancestors apparently knew a lot about. We're reduced to the legal age for drinking or the driver's license.

During the seventies a tremendously healthy discussion was going on as well in the U.S. around therapy, fairy tales, mythology, stages of growth and the meaning of initiation. I first heard Joseph Campbell talk in Toronto in 1975, and his book *The Hero with a Thousand Faces* was the bible of those discussions. He welded many different stories and myths together in a way that emphasized the heroic male, the young hero who leaves his village, fights various multiple-headed beings, gets a boon, and brings it back to the village. That was the initiation, so to speak, of the male hero. Do women have different stages of initiation? That wasn't discussed. Do artists have different stages of initiation? That wasn't discussed. Are there spiritual roads that involve the male learning grief? That wasn't discussed. Every book can contain only a small sliver of the vast field of mythology. Joseph Campbell opened the awareness of the link between mythology and initiation, and the discussions went on for years.

The Center for Healing Arts in Los Angeles, the Jung Center in San Francisco, and others asked me to tell fairy stories to groups of men and women and relate them to their ordinary life. The best stories for this purpose were from the Celtic clan, the Grimm Brothers, and the Russian collection by Afanasev. Two things became apparent. Women were much more willing to talk about their disasters and delights than the men. Most of the stories that we know— "Snow-White," "Snow-White and Rose-Red," "Rapunzel," "The Goose-Girl," "Thousandfurs," "Sleeping Beauty," "The Girl without Hands," "The Goose-Girl at the Well," "Maid Maleen" and so on— were of great interest to women. Secondly the men in these weekend seminars began to ask for a story that was specifically about the stages of masculine development. I found "Iron John," or "Eisenhans." I promised the men that I would do a book on that. Eight or nine years passed and the men kept saying, "Where is it?" Toward the end of that time, I had begun holding some seminars for men only. The first was at Lama Commune in New Mexico. Meanwhile Bill Moyers had heard about the work and was interested in doing a PBS program on it. When his program appeared, the work that I and many other teachers had been doing for ten or twelve years surfaced into public consciousness. It seemed to be just the right moment. The serious respect that had developed for Freudian and Jungian therapy meant that both men and women were willing to talk about some of their suffering in public, which people, particularly men, in my father's generation would never have done.

Men, we saw, took a deep interest in poetry and mythology. I thought it was beautiful. The media dismissed all this work as drumming and running in the woods, which reduced it to something ridiculous. I think the men's seminars were not threatening to the women's movement at all, but a lot of the critics of *Iron John* missed the point. Various horizontal forces have recently pulled the women's work away from feeling and pulled the men's work toward fundamentalism. Nevertheless, *The Christian Science Monitor* has estimated that there are a hundred thousand men in the New York-Connecticut-Massachusetts area participating in "leaderless men's groups." I still do a lot of teaching of men and, with Marion Woodman particularly, of groups of both men and women.

Interviewer: One quality of the men's work that surprised me was the amount of poetry that you and James Hillman and Michael Meade read or recited to the men's groups. The three of you gathered many of those poems in *The Rag and Bone Shop of the Heart*. In a sense, the men's work amounted to university teaching outside the university setting.

Bly: The media doesn't want to know that. The media has tried to paint things differently. The most powerful enemies of men's openness are the corporate men. Three or four years ago there were hundreds of posters in New York one spring saying, "You don't need to beat a drum or hug a tree to be a man." At the bottom: "Dewar's Whiskey." The corporate world dares to say to young men, knowing how much young men want to be men, that the only requirement for manhood is to become an alcoholic. That's disgusting. It's a tiny indication of the ammunition aimed at men who try to learn to talk or to feel. I think that the best result of the men's work so far, beyond the emphasis on grief, is the concept of mentoring, that is, providing older men for men who have no fathers. Bob Roberts has started up Project Return in New Orleans, and that project provides older ex-cons as mentors to young men coming out of prison. The return rate to prison for these young men is 15%, compared with 85% in the ordinary government programs. The major difference is the use of mentors in Bob Roberts's program.

9. Morning Poems

Interviewer: In 1998 you published a book called *Morning Poems*. Why did you take that title?

Bly: The poems in that book I wrote in bed, in the early morning. I took the plan from Bill Stafford, who, as you know, wrote a poem every morning for about forty years.

Interviewer: Did this morning work produce a different sort of poem for you?

Bly: Well, the mood is relaxed. That's nice. You say to yourself, "Well, this poem isn't going to be any good, but I'll write it anyway." The first detail that arrives is treated as if it were the end of a thread. When one follows that thread, whatever comes along is welcomed into the poem. It could be a three-legged dog or an old stick or a character out of *Madame Bovary*. Whatever it is, I'll welcome it into the poem. You can always take it out later. One has no idea where the poem is going. That's what I like. You're following a thread. Sometimes the flow goes easily—didn't Frost say, "a poem is like a piece of ice on a hot stove; it moves on its own melting"? It's like that. Stafford liked the Blake lines:

> I give you the end of a golden string.
> Only wind it into a ball;
> It will lead you in at heaven's gate
> Built into Jerusalem's wall.

Interviewer:: What are the stages of development from the initial impulse to the final poem? Could you give an idea of what that process might be like?

Bly: It's important to say that we're riding on little waves of language here, and the great genius of our language is its constant development of apt everyday phrases.

"It will lead you in" . . .to something. So already one has the suggestion that the thread is going to carry you into memory and maybe even beyond personal memory into cultural memory or religious memory. So the stakes are very high in a poem like this; there's very little will involved in it. There is a dancing among all the experiences you've ever had, and a dancing among the gifts you've received from your family, from the wider culture, from your reading. And then the hope is that you can begin to work yourself back into your own life.

Interviewer:: In these poems, form seems to be coming in more than it has in your work for many years. Quatrains are appearing.

Bly: Ah well. Maybe there's enough freedom in the associations, so that it's a relief to come back to form. Things move very swiftly in these poems—it's like hands doing a swift sketch. I didn't really plan the quatrains; they happened. One of our jobs these days, anyway, is to escape from free verse.

10. New Poems

Interviewer:: For at least three years you have been composing poems in a form related to the Islamic ghazal. Would you talk about those poems?

Bly: My son-in-law, Sunil Dutta, who was born in Jaipur, asked me to help him a few years ago to translate some poems of the Indian poet Ghalib, who lived in the 19th century and wrote in Urdu, which is a mixture of Persian and Hindi. I resisted doing more translations, but finally we got to work and finished thirty of his ghazals. Ghalib is wicked. He says:

> Their funeral date is already decided,
> But still people complain they can't sleep.

The ghazal form, which usually contains from three to fifteen stanzas, has two remarkable characteristics. The poet can change the landscape in each stanza. One *sher*, or stanza, can be a love poem, the next can be wisdom literature, the third a complaint about the poet's private life. A second characteristic is that the poet never states the subject of the poem. In our tradition the poet may start, "Come live with me and be my love," and he or she will stay with that argument. A poem may begin: "Something there is that doesn't love a wall." Frost will add anecdotes, arguments, images until the subject is fulfilled.

Interviewer: But Frost brings many moods into a single poem.

Bly: He does, yes. We know that Frost believes there's some force in the universe that wants walls to come down. That conviction is deeply inside Frost. But also deeply inside Frost is a sense that we are somehow abandoned and left to live in a really lonely, dangerous universe. Also inside Frost is the recognition that a feeling of connection between two people may be so strong that when they walk up a mountain, the buck that looks at them will feel it. Those perceptions are spoken out in three separate poems in Frost; but in the ghazal tradition, all three of those would go inside the same poem.

Interviewer: So I gather the reader has more to do. When the theme of the poem is not stated, that leaves more work for the listener. Probably it encourages him or her to listen a little more carefully than we might when the poem is recited.

Bly: Yes, that's true. The language of the ghazal is deliberately complicated as well. In general, the ghazal belongs to a cultured poetry with many references to other poems and poets. Each image is an exaggeration, one might say, which suggests the opposite. So the ghazal stanza provides a kind of chamber in which opposite things can be said.

Interviewer: Did the ghazal poem come out of an aristocratic world?

Bly: The word *ghazal* means love poem, and it seems to have started as a love poem in Arabic. The form was elaborated by the Persians. The ghazal was developed still further in the twelfth century in Persia and in India. But the form is still used all over the Islamic world. Some of this poetry comes from Sufis who don't own anything. Sanai says, "If you can't go without food for five days, stop bragging about being a Sufi." So that's not aristocratic. It's not common, either. What are you asking about this poem?

Interviewer: Well, I think the ghazals you've mentioned assume a lot of learning.

Bly: That's true, they do. We need more poems like that. What's the use of having a rich literary and cultural past, and then ignoring it?

Interviewer: So the ghazal is not free verse.

Bly: Not at all! I've mentioned that the ghazal often makes a leap to a new subject matter with each new stanza; that is itself a form of wildness. The ghazal has massive forms of discipline, however, as if to balance that wildness. For example, there is the *radif* element. The first two lines announce a *radif* word such as *night* or a word meaning "enough for us." Every couplet in the poem will end with that same word. The interesting thing is that whenever *night* arrives, it is as if a whole world comes with that word. In this way, it's a little different than rhyme. Hafez has a poem in which the repeating Persian word can be translated as "enough for us." "The shadow of a tall cypress in a meadow is enough for us." And then he goes on and says things like:

> You have seen the cash flow and the world's suffering.
> If that profit and loss is not enough for you, for us it's enough.

And by us he's referring to a whole community, so that in a way, the community appears each time the line ends: "for us it's enough." The reader knows that a word is going to be repeated, and is delighted to see that it's slightly different in each of the couplets. There is some rhyming too, and of course meter as well, but the *radif* is the most unusual element to us.

***Interviewer*:** Would you recite one?

***Bly*:**

> Some love to watch the sea bushes appearing at dawn,
> To see night fall from the goose's wings, and to hear
> The conversations the night sea has with the dawn.
>
> If we can't find Heaven, there are always bluejays.
> Now you know why I spent my twenties crying.
> Cries are required from those who wake disturbed at dawn.
>
> Adam was called in to name the Red-Winged
> Blackbirds, the Diamond Rattlers, and the Ring-Tailed
> Raccoons washing God in the streams at dawn.
>
> Centuries later, the Mesopotamian gods,
> All curls and ears, showed up; behind them the Generals
> With their blue-coated sons who will die at dawn.

Those grasshopper-eating hermits were so good
To stay all day in the cave; but it is also sweet
To see the fenceposts gradually appear at dawn.

People in love with the setting stars are right
To adore the baby who smells of the stable, but we know
That even the setting stars will disappear at dawn.

The writer jumps on a new horse with each stanza, one could say. But then the rider gets off the horse at the end of every stanza and takes the reader's hand. It makes for a wildness that still has care for the reader, almost courtesy.

***Interviewer*:** You decided to change the usual two-line Persian stanza to a three-line stanza. Why did you do that?

***Bly*:** The line that poets use most often in both Persian and Arabic tends to be sixteen or eighteen syllables. So if you have two eighteen-syllable lines, you really have thirty-six syllables. By contrast, the typical line in English, in the sonnets, for example, is ten syllables. A line in English becomes unwieldy if it's extended into eighteen syllables. By adopting three eleven- or twelve-syllable lines, you end up with about thirty-six syllables. I think the Islamic writers felt that thirty-six syllables is a useful and completed unit of expressiveness. That's why I went to three lines.

***Interviewer*:** The poem suggests that wildness can stay with us as we get older. Perhaps the ghazal's particular merging of wildness and form is more appropriate to a 70 year old than to a 20 year old.

***Bly*:** It's good of you to say that.

II. Coda

***Interviewer*:** Did you ever think of going into a university?

***Bly*:** My idea of a poet was formed in 1950! I wanted to be independent of universities, as William Carlos Williams was, or Wallace Stevens or Eliot. Part of my reluctance was probably arrogance. But I do write best when I have a lot of time alone. I still say to my wife sometimes, "You know, I really should have joined a university. Then I could have one of those little white houses in some New England town, and there would be a sun porch and a salary; and when I got to school there would be these happy faces longing to see me!"

"Ah," she says, "You would have gotten fired anyway because you never keep your mouth shut!" That's probably true. Maybe I'm happier outside the university than I would be inside.

***Interviewer*:** You've done some teaching lately for Galway Kinnell at NYU, and last year and this year for the Bennington writing program.

***Bly*:** Yes, I taught "The Craft of Poetry" for Galway's program one year. I'd see the writing students from six to eight on a Monday. I'd talk about the Seven Holy Vowels, or read Stevens or Marvell to them and go out high as a kite at eight. I do like also the non-residential writing programs like Liam Rector's at Bennington. The writers, often parents or working people, exchange letters with their teachers regularly and then come in to Bennington for a few days twice a year. Don Hall and I are "poets in residence," so we can do whatever we like. Don and I can spend some time together, meet younger writers, and hear some lectures.

***Interviewer*:** You and Don Hall have been friends for years?

***Bly*:** Donald Hall and I have been sending poems back and forth twice a week for forty years. At one time, we had a 48-hour rule: the other had to answer within 48 hours. My generation did a lot with letters. Galway Kinnell and Louis Simpson and Don and I and James Wright would often send five- and six-page typed letters commenting on and arguing with each others' poems. I'm amazed we had the time for that. Tranströmer and I exchanged hundreds of letters. The gist of it is that no one writes alone: One needs a community.

—The interviewer is Francis Quinn

AFTERWORD

REMEMBERING ROBERT BLY

Jane Hirshfield

The literary landscape into which I and my generation of poets came of age was Robert Bly's landscape. It included, along with Robert himself, Neruda, Vallejo, and Lorca; Mirabai, Kabir, and Rumi; Rilke, Tranströmer, Goethe, Hölderlin, and Celan. Poets I, and countless others, learned of not least because Robert and the circle of early poet-friends who visited his Minnesota farm — William Duffy, James Wright, others — swung open the gate to that larger world. They did this through their translations, through their own poems, and through also their friendships-- with one another, and with poets from every corner of map, language, and time.

Robert's story might be traced as a lifelong search for friends. Some helped him build fences and a shared dictionary of poems; some had set their words down centuries before, in Chinese mountains and North Indian forests; some embodied the figure addressed by Sufis as "Friend." The search for friendship was also part of Robert's great gift for community-making. He wanted to gather with others who wanted, as he did, the wild, hidden ores held in old stories and long understandings released newly by a first-hand telling and first-hand naming. He wanted conferences, meetings, festivals, the community of a magazine's writers and readers; he wanted others performing with him on a stage, often with sitar and tabla. He wanted, too, in his poems, prose, interviews, letters, to find his own friendship with existence itself– to forge a great, yes-saying agreement to whatever life asks and brings.

Saying yes doesn't mean staying passive before injustice, selfishness, willed blindness to others' suffering. The landscape I and my generation of poets came into was one as well of civil rights and anti-war demonstrations; of growing environmental awareness; of small presses' mimeograph-ink or sometimes letterpress publishing; of letters to the editor and full-length books rebuking, praising, badgering, instructing — again, ground Robert Bly helped lay open. Ploughing snowy fields may appear an image quiet, local, comically futile, but the crop that comes from doing it is real. Naming what is ignored or kept hidden leads to new kinds of envisioning. Also, to ethics: to the recognition of what needs repair and not staying silent before it. This work of tikkun olam — the repair of the world — Robert took on all his life.

Over his six or so decades in poetry's, the psyche's, and society's service, Robert summoned hidden molecular orbitings, birds, fish, camels, myths, the work of the Jungian shadow, the whirling velocities and flamboyant gestures of spirit. He wrote, he translated, he assembled anthologies that altered this world's understanding and our human understanding of how to live in it. Among his root-stock contributions were also his teachings about what poems might do and how they might do it: the seven holy vowels, the leaping image. Robert did not claim to discover these things–he found them in the poems he loved. But his gift for memorable naming and his apostolic advocacy for their importance shifted American poetry's course.

Robert was, first and last, a poet. His poems hold the heart's and the world's broken-open suffering, and hold also the heart's and world's ineradicable radiance. Robert loved silence all his life and knew it was not sufficient– knew that a life, to be full, also needs voicing, needs dancing. Compression of spirit and constriction seemed a physical and unbearable source of pain for him, in his own life, in the life of others. And so, the poems cultivate and farm, they graft and hybridize and prune, seeking new expressions and new reminders of bedrock knowledge. They fold up their wings of delight and kneel, proposing marriage between earthly realms and those transcendent. Robert believed wisdom possible and findable. Poetic form became his late ally in wisdom's service: after a lifetime of writing in free verse's organic-form ways, he turned in his last books toward a three-line, ghazal-echoing stanza to set down some maps to knowledge sayable in no other way. In the Urdu, ghazals are written in lengthy couplets. Robert's three-line choice for the form in English was like his relationship to the old wisdoms in general: it both bows to the past and gives it new shape in the present.

The body was also always present in Robert's work and in how he spoke it aloud in public. He dressed for effect, his scarves and vests close to what we would now call gender-fluid. Whenever he recited a poem or taught about poetry — almost always from memory, almost always repeating for emphasis certain thoughts or lines or full poems — his whole body recited. His hands, especially, became tambourine, castanet, dancers, conductors.

We met first when I was asked to introduce Robert at a Pacifica Radio station benefit reading in Berkeley. From the moment we each were draped backstage in big maroon gift shawls, we became friends. He invited me to present at Great Mother gatherings on both coasts. If he knew I was in the audience when he read, he'd call me up onto the stage to say a poem or two. We once co-led a weekend at The Omega Institute, near Woodstock, and at one point found ourselves debating the capacity of a plain white soup bowl to hold not only the ordinary but the full range of psyche and spirit. At the time, I thought Robert was only pretending to believe that impossible, but he later described the conversation as having changed his views. A few years later yet, when Beacon Press asked him to bring out a long-set-aside project, a book-length translation of Mirabai's poetry, he refused to do it unless I joined him, insisting, over my protests, on two introductions of equal length and that we contribute an identical number of poems. One poem, we inadvertently both translated — so differently, it's in the book twice. To my knowledge, no one has ever noticed.

I like to imagine Robert and Mirabai meeting–a conversation of two flowering gardens, bees and hummingbirds traveling between them. When I find myself wanting reminding of what prose can be — as much as what poems can — I sometimes reread Robert's book introductions and essays on craft. His descriptions feel to me lightning rods, summoning from every direction of earth, sky, heart-mind, and tongue, the pure electricity of unlikely, unerring connection. Even in prose, his images, thoughts, music, and metaphors have their own eyes, cast their own light. Robert praises other poets with the surety of a river channel that has been carved by something beyond itself. In his teaching, translating, and anthologizing of others' poems, he was transmitting the works that had made him who he was– a person of altering delight, altering grief, altering darkness. He thirsted for and made transformation. In a world of ceaseless losses, injustices, blindness, and limitations, he found also the miracles of loaves and fishes, the grapes turned to wine. My favorite of the late poems' statements: "I am a man in love with the setting stars."

When I last saw Robert at his home, he'd become a person as he must have been when very young: more silent. When he and his beloved wife Ruth came down the front walk from their house in the Minneapolis snow, they walked arm in arm, a steadying whose anchoring appeared — from the outside — still mutual and equal. His posture was upright as always, but softened. His sweater, dark blue, flecked with small white snowflakes, or perhaps stars, was banded at the neck with the bright red of a woodpecker's crown. He loved and was loved, and knew that his work in the larger world was closing.

In the days after learning of Robert's death, I kept returning to a strangely unwavering image: that he should be honored as certain great warriors once were, placed in a boat set aflame and released onto the Great Lakes' dark waters, leaving this world in a final theatrical blazing up, with all the earth's elements in attendance. All his life, Robert had carried the instinct for drama. In a phone-taken video of him saying "Keeping Our Small Boat Afloat" at his last public reading, one foot moves with his words, still dancing, though a metal walking cane rests against his chair. His voice falters a little early on, but strengthens by the close into the old deep channel. He knows the poem's ending nails it. You can see and hear it yourself, on YouTube, if you like:

https://www.youtube.com/watch?v=Pq8bQ0mjZ54

Robert's voice, ideas, and ground-badger-stubbon allegiance to the speaking soul, to the earth itself, and to the lineage of those who have walked its ground before us, have entered the deep aquifers of language. I am grateful to Thomas R. Smith and White Pine Press for the chance to revisit in this book's pages some of the source-springs, and to drink in Robert's words the clear water that rises directly — astonishingly, originally — out of the rocky cliff and dancing meadow he himself was.

Thomas R. Smith is an internationally published poet, essayist, editor, and teacher living in western Wisconsin. He worked as Robert Bly's personal assistant from 1990 until the time of Bly's death in 2022. He has edited three earlier books on Bly's work, *Walking Swiftly, Robert Bly in This World* (with James P. Lenfestey), and *Airmail: The Letters of Robert Bly and Tomas Tranströmer*. His ten poetry collections include, most recently, *Windy Day at Kabekona: New and Selected Prose Poems, Storm Island*, and *Medicine Year*. He has also published a prose work, *Poetry on the Side of Nature: Writing the Nature Poem as an Act of Survival.* He teaches at the Loft Literary Center in Minneapolis and posts poems and essays at www.thomasrsmithpoet.com.

Acknowledgments:

"Being a Lutheran Boy-God in Minnesota" first appeared in *Growing Up in Minnesotas: Ten Writers Remember Their Childhoods,* Chester G. Anderson, ed., University of Minnesota Press, Minneapolis, 1976.

"When Literary Life Was Still Piled Up in a Few Places" first appeared in *A Community of Writers: Paul Engle and the Iowa Writers' Workshop,* Robert Dana, ed., University of Iowa Press, Iowa City, IA, 1999.

"Snowbanks North of the House" first appeared in *Poetry East* #43, *Origins: Poets on the Composition Process,* Richard Jones, ed., DePaul University, Chicago, 1996.

"Six Disciplines That Intensity Poetry" first appeared in *The Thousands, No. 1,* The Thousands Press, Minneapolis, MN, 2001.

"What the Image Can Do" first appeared in *American Poetry: Wildness and Domesticity,* Harper & Row, New York, 1990. An earlier version appeared in *Claims for Poetry,* ed. Donald Hall, The University of Michigan Press, Ann Arbor, 1982.

"Educating the Rider and the Horse" first appeared in *American Poetry: Wildness and Domesticity,* Harper & Row, New York, 1990. An earlier version appeared as "Form That Is Neither In Nor Out" in *Of Solitude and Silence: Writings on Robert Bly,* ed. Richard Jones and Kate Daniels, Beacon Press, Boston, 1981.

"A Playful Look at Form" first appeared in *American Poetry: Wildness and Domesticity,* Harper & Row, New York, 1990. An earlier version appeared as "Reflections on the Origins of Poetic Form" in *A "Field" Guide to Contemporary Poetry and Poetics,* ed. Stuart Friebert and David Young, Longman, New York and London, 1980.

"Form in Society and in the Poem" first appeared in *American Poetry: Wildness and Domesticity,* Harper & Row, New York, 1990. An earlier version appeared as "Poetry in an Age of Expansion" in *The Nation,* April 22nd, 1961.

"Praising the Seven Holy Vowels" first appeared in *The Hungry Mind Review,* No. 42, St. Paul, Minnesota, 1997.

"A Week of Ghazals" first appeared in *The Minneapolis StarTribune,* Minneapolis, MN, December 3-9, 2001.

"The Paris Review Interview" first appeared in *The Paris Review,* No. 154, 2000.

White Pine Press is grateful to the following individuals whose extraordinary support and funding made publication of *The Garden Entrusted to Me* possible.

Thomas Beaudoin
Thomas Buckley
Helene Cardona
Wyn Cooper
Geri Grossman
Ian Haight
Wyllhart Halle
James Jay
Stephen Kuusisto
Tom Lagasse
Nancy Lagomarsino
Jessie Lendennie
Lenfestey Family Foundation
Joseph Millar
Dick Olsen
Rachael Resch
Nicole Spencer
Thom Tommaro
George Uschold
Randi Ward